NOT LIKE ANY
OTHER BOOK

NOT LIKE ANY OTHER BOOK

Interpreting the Bible

PETER MASTERS

THE WAKEMAN TRUST, LONDON

NOT LIKE ANY OTHER BOOK

THE WAKEMAN TRUST
(UK Registered Charity)

Website: www.wakemantrust.org

UK Registered Office
38 Walcot Square
London SE11 4TZ

US Office
300 Artino Drive
Oberlin, OH 44074-1263

ISBN 1 870855 43 4

Cover design by Andrew Owen

Printed by Stephens & George, Merthyr Tydfil, UK

To the great army of
Reformation tradition preachers,
commentators and theologians from the past,
including Reformers, Puritans, instruments of mighty
awakenings and of worldwide missionary
initiatives, who knew far better
how to interpret the Bible
than we do today.

Contents

1

A Silent Revolution

THE ELDERS and deacons of a small but well-established evangelical church – it could be in Britain or the USA – are meeting to consider a shortlist of names for the vacant pastorate of their church. The most likely and available candidates are two who recently completed training at well-respected seminaries. The discussion of the officers, all astute and spiritually-minded men, is chiefly about the qualities required in a pastor, but there is something they do not know about the two candidates that could upset everything. They are not aware that at their seminaries, although soundly evangelical and Calvinistic, a radical departure from once-orthodox teaching has occurred.

The officers have no idea of the revolution that has taken place in so many sound seminaries and Bible colleges all over the world in recent decades concerning the interpretation of the Scriptures. Why should they suspect that well-known bastions of Truth would be furnishing the minds of aspiring pastors with sub-scriptural ideas about interpretation? Yet it is happening. It is a painful fact that views evolved from liberal thinking (and opposed in times past by Victorian evangelicals) are now authoritatively taught even at fine seminaries, creating a tremendous gulf between the *modern approach* (as we shall call it) and the methods followed by the overwhelming majority of sound preachers since the time of the Reformation. Seminarians often receive an excellent education in biblical languages, systematic theology, Bible history, and possibly in pastoral theology also, but in exegesis and exposition of Scripture, perhaps the most important course of all, they are being severely let down.

This book will try to show what has gone wrong, and what we believe to be the right and biblical way. We will also provide examples of how the right way alone unlocks the full message of the Word of God. This is not only a vital topic for preachers, very many of whom will warmly identify with what is said here, but it is equally important for all Christians loyal to the Bible. If church officers had been made aware of this trend years ago, their inevitable disquiet might well have forced the sounder colleges to rethink their position and resist the new ideas.

On a completely different front, if believers generally had been given a clearer view of the principles of Bible interpretation years ago, we might never have seen the crazy extremes of the charismatic movement, which all defy these principles. Later chapters will round up examples of mistakes which would not have occurred if the Bible's own rules had been followed. All should know the fundamentals of Bible interpretation, and what is going wrong today.

The new philosophy of interpretation started to enter faithful Bible colleges in the 1960s, greatly accelerating in influence in the 1980s, until now it commands the majority of classrooms. Many of its teachers go as far as to say that the Bible must be interpreted like any other book. However much we believe in the Bible's divine inspiration, we should study it in more or less the same way that we study human literature, namely, in a scientific, objective, analytical way. Scripture must no longer be treated as a uniquely divine book with its own distinctive rules for interpretation.

Along with those who opposed this scheme when it was first advocated by nineteenth-century Bible-denying liberals, we say it is humanistic and anti-spiritual in essence, and will seriously hinder preachers from seeing the vital spiritual and pastoral messages intended by the Lord in His Word. In short, it is destructive to real preaching, as evidenced by the rather dry and pastorally insipid commentaries written by scholars who work in accordance with this approach.

Of course, what we are calling the modern approach varies somewhat from textbook to textbook, but the ideas we shall set out are the general position. We will summarise the modern approach shortly, but we must first ask why sincere evangelical educators have followed earlier liberal theologians down this dismal road. Scholarly evangelical advocates of the modern approach usually express their dismay and concern about preachers who interpret the Bible in an entirely allegorical and devotional way. They want to train men to undertake a serious scientific evaluation of any passage they preach from, and they think that the modern approach will achieve this, but cannot see that it destroys the Bible's own rules for its interpretation. It is like giving a person a fatal dose of poison to cure an illness, or putting a straitjacket on someone merely suffering from tics and twitches.

By following the modern approach the expositor's skill for discerning the spiritual content of the text will be slight, leading to his applications being light and his presentation of God and His purposes shallow. The modern approach may be suitable for the study of secular literature, although even this is questionable. Many of the great writers and most playwrights have an underlying (though not hidden) meaning in their works, and as schoolchildren we were expected to grasp the subtext of plays of Shakespeare, and even of *Alice in Wonderland.* We would have earned no marks for handing in assignments insisting that the surface, literal sense of the author was the only meaning. Teachers of the modern approach seem to want the Bible to have *less* significance than secular literature, treating it more like a science textbook. The reality is that the Bible is not like any other book, and must be handled with awe and reverence in accordance with its uniqueness and its own special rules.

Modern approach teachers have become obsessed with the idea that the meaning of the Bible is obscured to us today both by the culture of the writers, and also by our own culture. They massively exaggerate these problems, rejecting the time-honoured view that God has spoken plainly in a way that people will comprehend in all generations. They have virtually swept away the good old Protestant affirmation that individual Christians may read and understand the Bible. Creating countless imagined difficulties, the modern approach has borrowed heavily from liberal theologians and their notions about the philosophy of language to construct elaborate stages of literary and cultural analysis to 'understand' the text. Meanwhile, nearly all *biblical* and *spiritual* approaches have been abandoned.

By the time of his graduation today's theological student, trained to work within restrictive technical rules lacking any spiritual dimension, resembles a curiously trained athlete who has one immensely powerful leg and another which is shrunken and wasted. In what event could such an athlete compete? When the would-be preacher leaves college with his grossly unbalanced hermeneutical limbs, he must discover for himself how to rightly handle the Word, and his success or failure as a preacher will depend upon this.

His training in biblical languages will be a great asset to him, and let us hope other courses also, but for the expounding of the

Bible he has been taught hopeless liberal ideas that will ruin him if he does not recognise them and replace them with better ones.

It is undeniable that if such preachers as George Whitefield and C. H. Spurgeon had applied the methods of interpretation advocated today in the modern approach they would never have been able to preach their magnificent sermons. (Nor would Calvin or Matthew Henry have written their commentaries, to name only two of the great army of old writers who never used anything resembling the humanistic rules of the modern approach.) We must urgently return to the level of respect for the inspired Word that gave rise to the sermons of the Reformers, the Puritans, the pulpit worthies of great awakenings, and other eras of outstanding, Christ-honouring preaching.

This writer, happily, is by no means a lone voice in these matters, for thousands of pastors the world over view with amazement the highly limiting and Spirit-quenching tendencies of present-day interpretation classes. We also know seminary professors and lecturers who shake their heads in dismay at what the hermeneutics department is doing. (Some have issued excellent books urging preachers to find the real purpose of the text, and to see Christ in His own Word.) And yet the modern approach is everywhere.

These may seem to be shockingly exaggerated and unwelcome assertions, but once readers have seen the coldly secular rules of the modern approach, they also will be horrified at the extent of the departure from former evangelical ways. This writer hopes that many elders and deacons like those pictured at the beginning of this chapter will be alerted to these dangers before being confronted with the weighty responsibility of guiding a church in the appointing of a new pastor. At least they will be able to determine whether a seminary graduate has discerned the errors, and begun to research a better direction.

For all that we have said, the wrong claims of the modern

approach teachers have some usefulness, because their errors serve to focus our minds on what is right. Their fundamental statements are so wrong that they clarify our *opposite* expression of true interpretation. Just as the saying, 'like any other book', must be turned around, and expressed as '*not* like any other book', so every foundational principle of the modern approach must be completely restated to say the opposite, as we shall show in these pages. Only by doing this shall we see and know the Bible's own rules for its interpretation. This is about the liberation of the message of the Word of God from the shackles of restrictive human meddling.

2

Danger Beneath the Surface

IF CUSTOM OFFICERS board a ship in harbour or comb through the contents of a truck straight off the ferry, they know they have a search on their hands. If they see bags of flour stacked up in front of them, they remove them one by one to find what they are looking for – bags of cocaine and heroin lying amidst the innocent flour. These, of course, are the truly significant items, and the real business of the importers. So it is with the modern approach to interpretation. The significant, pivotal, dynamic elements are not the obvious, surface things, but the ideas that underlie them and profoundly influence everything.

The modern approach seems to beguile some evangelical seminary instructors for the very reason that its main system of steps seems reasonable, but throughout it is horribly skewed by ideas diametrically opposed to the Bible's own statements about interpretation. On the surface the modern approach is typically presented as five or six stages (even up to ten!) of interpretation along the lines of the following headings. (Don't worry about the technical terms, these stages are like the bags of flour and we will not discuss them to any extent.) (1) Historical, cultural and contextual analysis; (2) syntactical analysis; (3) literary analysis; (4) theological analysis; and (5) homiletical analysis. There would be great merit in these steps if they were not made subservient to liberal ideas, and also made absurdly complicated. Strewn through these steps are six unbiblical and fatal flaws – the bags of cocaine and heroin – and it is these that we must challenge. We admit, our illustration about hidden packets of drugs is not altogether fair or appropriate, because while these flaws are not usually presented as the key points by modern approach teachers, they make no secret of them. Here is a list of the principles of the modern approach which we must expose:–

(1) The sole task of the expositor is to understand the literal sense consciously intended by the original human author to be fully understood by his contemporary hearers. There is no other meaning to a text.

(2) Every passage of Scripture has but a single sense or meaning, and no other.

(3) The interpreter must not bring to a passage any religious opinions, expectations or presuppositions.

(4) No biblical doctrine or other text may be allowed to throw light on a passage unless it was known to the original human author. (So the New Testament must not be used to throw light on the Old.)

(5) The interpreter must never allegorise or spiritualise a passage for this is utterly reprehensible. (Poor Matthew Henry, not to mention a host of Puritans!)

(6) An application for today must be derived strictly from the human author's intended meaning.

Unbelievable as it may seem to many readers, this is what is being taught today (in part or in whole) from the leading textbooks on the subject used in very many evangelical seminaries and Bible colleges, and each 'principle' is the very opposite of the truth.

The writer has surveyed a range of evangelical textbooks in favour of the modern approach as they have emerged over the last 30 years, and first wrote published articles on this theme over 20 years ago. While there is variation (and contradiction) between these books, they all reach fairly similar conclusions. A couple of examples will show the trends.

One widely influential author stands out for his fluent, energetic and militant style, going out on a limb on a number of matters. One admires his lively prose, but there is a strange characteristic about all his work – not untypical of books promoting the modern approach. He sees only two kinds of interpreter-preacher. On the one hand there are superficial allegorisers, justly denounced for overuse of their imaginations, and on the other there are modern approach interpreters. Strangely, the overwhelming majority of preachers in the Reformation tradition have disappeared.

The Reformers, the Puritans, the eighteenth and nineteenth-century pulpit worthies have all gone, and the reader is given a stark choice of style between crude allegorising and the cold, unspiritual analysing of the modern approach. Where is C. H. Spurgeon whose sermons have been more widely read and admired than those of any other preacher? Where are the likes of William Carey, and the luminaries of the 'golden age' of Baptist expansion? Where are the Victorian pulpiteers and their successors? The style of interpretation adopted by the historical mainstream of sound preachers is not so much as acknowledged.

The most widely used textbook by a professing evangelical prolif-erates rarified technical terms to such an extent that most students must be amazed and confounded. The history of interpretation is dragged out through protracted discussion of the way-out theories of non-evangelical philosophers, and literary analysis is pursued to a preposterous degree. Once again, absent from the author's historical survey is any appreciation of the mainstream practice of preachers from the Reformation until the 1960s, and also any recognition of the interpretive rules provided within the Bible.

Another, more recent, large textbook comes from three seminary professors who clearly hold the biblical text in high regard and maintain a careful and gentlemanly tone throughout. They make generous allowances here and there for the 'traditional' view of interpretation, and go as far as to draw back from a total ban on presuppositions in interpretation. However, these authors also see no rules of interpretation in the Bible itself, and with numerous quotations from liberal theologians, and massively over-elaborate definitions and expansions of literary terms, they promote the very ideas we are challenging in this book.

It is surely significant that no modern approach author as far as we know has any published sermons to his name, which is a pity as we, as well as prospective students, would like to see the results achieved by those who teach in this field. We have a few sample outlines in their textbooks, and we also have several commentaries from among them, but no sermons delivered to real people. Would they really invest the very many hours of technical analysis they advocate for the preparation of a sermon? Would they produce *spiritual* meaning and application for their hearers? It is hard to imagine so, given the restrictive nature of the methods they advance. How would their messages compare with those of past pulpit worthies who knew nothing of the elaborate procedures taught in their classes? But let us move on to see what the modern ideas about interpretation amount to.

3

The Wholly-Human Bible
Only the human author's intended meaning allowed
(The first defective rule)

WE OFTEN speak of the grammatical-historical principle, which came out of the Reformation and says we must show unflagging respect for the grammatical sense of a passage, viewed in its historical context. In other words, we must base everything we do on the plain sense of the text, and surely no one disputes that. But today's writers mean much more than that, for they have tightened up the old definition to say the following:

> **The sole task of the expositor is to understand the literal sense consciously intended by the original human author to be fully understood by his contemporary hearers.**

This definition makes the Bible just like any other book. It is rationalistic and anti-spiritual, and is particularly deadening for the Old Testament. It means that an original Old Testament author perfectly understood his meaning, and so did his hearers, and there is nothing more profound to be searched out from the text; no deeper pastoral intention, only the face value of the bare words. As it is sometimes expressed, the human author never spoke better than he knew. We are not to think (according to this theory) that *God* wrote every passage with us in mind, and that there are Old Testament events which parallel present-day spiritual experiences, yielding pastoral applications intended by the Lord for us. With the modern approach, application is something that must be added on by the preacher.

Advocates of the modern approach often claim that Calvin and other Reformers taught this idea, but it is not true. By selective quotation they make the great expositor say such things, but these are phoney claims, latching on to the concern of all the Reformers to oppose the wildly allegorical, multiple-level meanings proposed by medieval Catholic clergy. They greatly exaggerate Calvin's comments, and say nothing about his insistence that there are spiritual parallels to be recognised in the Old Testament, placed there by the Lord. (A classic statement of Calvin's appears on pages 55-56.)

The *old* approach calls for the plain, grammatical sense to be given first crack of the whip, and to be carefully honoured even when a spiritual parallel for the church of Christ is evident. Understanding the plain sense is the first, vital step in the expounding of a passage, but not by any means the *sole* task of the interpreter, for when it is, the straitjacket is firmly in place to bind and limit the interpreter's understanding of the Word. We must give the closest attention to the literal meaning of the passage in its historical context, but because the Bible is not like any other book, this does not exhaust the work of interpretation.

We deny that the human authors always understood everything of the message that God gave them, for they were given words from the very mind of God, and were frequently moved to write far more Truth than they appreciated. We learn from *1 Peter 1.10-12* that the inspired writers of the Old Testament studied their own words just as we search the Scriptures today. No doubt they understood what they had written up to a point, but became 'Bible students' when they wished to grasp the detailed implications of the message God had channelled through them. Peter says –

> 'Of which salvation the prophets have inquired and searched diligently, who prophesied of the grace that should come unto you: searching what, or what manner of time the Spirit of Christ which was in them did signify, when it testified beforehand the sufferings of Christ, and the glory that should follow. Unto whom it was revealed, that not unto themselves, but unto us they did minister the things, which are now reported unto you by them that have preached the gospel unto you with the Holy Ghost sent down from heaven; which things the angels desire to look into.'

Supporters of the modern approach protest that this text only refers to the *time* of Christ's coming, as though the prophets knew everything else, but this is shallow reasoning. Peter says they searched *what* the Spirit signified as well as the time. (The 'what' refers to what person or what circumstances.) Even the angels, with their mighty intellects, did not understand exactly how Christ would purchase salvation until they looked from Heaven and saw His work fulfilled.

Prophecy is an obvious example of messages given to inspired authors which were often beyond their comprehension. Some prophecies would never be grasped until the time of their fulfilment.

However, the original writers' limitations go far beyond this, for their words contain types[*] of Christ, along with many pastoral instructions for the church age, that they would not necessarily have discerned. The two disciples on the road to Emmaus *(Luke 24)* would undoubtedly have known their literal Old Testament history, as recorded by the human authors, but they listened with amazement and growing joy as the risen Lord taught them the real meaning, saying:

---

[*]Types are persons, objects or events that serve as prophetic illustrations or likenesses of New Testament fulfilments.

> 'O fools, and slow of heart to believe all that the prophets have spoken: ought not Christ to have suffered these things, and to enter into his glory? And beginning at Moses and all the prophets, he expounded unto them in all the scriptures the things concerning himself' *(Luke 24.25-27).*

Christ in the Old Testament was also central to the preaching of Paul, who (in *Acts 26.22-23*) convinces well-instructed Jewish leaders of . . .

> 'none other things than those which the prophets and Moses did say should come: that Christ should suffer, and that he should be the first that should rise from the dead.'

Much of the Old Testament is a narrative of events, and the purpose of the original penmen was to accurately record what the Holy Spirit inspired. They would need to study the text for themselves to see the prefigurations of Christ's work – clear enough to the eye of faith. A. W. Pink summed up the entire Puritan tradition perfectly when he noted:

> 'The Old Testament Scriptures are something more than a compilation of historical records; something more than a system of social and religious legislation; something more than a code of ethics. The Old Testament Scriptures are fundamentally a stage on which is shown forth in vivid symbolism and ritualism the whole plan of redemption. The events recorded were actual occurrences, yet they were also typical prefigurations.'

In *Romans 15.4* the apostle Paul gives a sweeping yet authoritative description of the real purpose of the Old Testament, saying:

> 'For whatsoever things were written aforetime were written for our learning, that we through patience and comfort of the scriptures might have hope.'

Everything without exception written in the Old Testament was written for us today, as well as for those days. God spoke with us in mind. So the interpreter must not confine himself to the bare history, but he must see the gracious doctrines, views of Christ, and exhortations to patience and comfort from the examples and promises of every book. This is not done by looking for a vague moral, or concocting from our own imagination a hazy analogy from Bible history for present-day application, but by discerning the pastoral message that God clearly intended to be inherent in the events. It is not possible to do this if we choose to take a tunnel-vision view of the immediate, literal sense intended by the human author. We must step back and see that the historical books provide practical demonstrations and illustrations of the ways of God towards man (as well as much implicit doctrinal revelation).

It is often said that those people whose affairs were recorded in the historical books were the unwitting actors on the stage of God's Word, experiencing events often representing deliverance, conversion, God's way of responding to human faith or unbelief, the believer's pilgrimage, and even the Lord's design of the New Testament church, and many other matters. God proved Himself to them, and through them, to us. Supremely, many passages speak of Christ, but we would never know it if we followed the modern approach. The presence of lessons about Christ together with parallels of the spiritual life is confirmed in *1 Corinthians 10.1-4* (considered more fully a little later).

> 'Moreover, brethren, I would not that ye should be ignorant, how that all our fathers were under the cloud, and all passed through the sea; and were all baptized unto Moses in the cloud and in the sea; and did all eat the same spiritual meat; and did all drink the same spiritual drink: for they drank of that spiritual Rock that followed them: and that Rock was Christ.'

At once we see that the modern approach is set against the Bible's own rules for its interpretation. While Paul does not want us to be ignorant of the divine purposes behind the narrative, the modern approach teachers want us to close our minds to them.

Here are some examples of where the New Testament tells us that there is a deeper significance to an Old Testament passage than the bare words shut up in the context of the generation that heard them. The first is from *1 Corinthians 9.7-10*:

> 'Who goeth a warfare any time at his own charges? who planteth a vineyard, and eateth not of the fruit thereof? or who feedeth a flock, and eateth not of the milk of the flock? Say I these things as a man? or saith not the law the same also? For it is written in the law of Moses, Thou shalt not muzzle the mouth of the ox that treadeth out the corn. Doth God take care for oxen? Or saith he it altogether for our sakes? For our sakes, no doubt, this is written: that he that ploweth should plow in hope; and that he that thresheth in hope should be partaker of his hope.'

What right does Paul have to say (in the verses that follow) that the law about the care of working animals also covers the support of priests, and later the ministers of the Gospel? He does not merely quote the law as an illustration, but states firmly that the old law expressly covers the support of Gospel ministers. He does not change the literal meaning of the words used by Moses, as an allegoriser might, but shows that they reasonably cover far more than at first appears.

In commenting on Paul's question, 'Doth God take care for oxen?' Martin Luther replied, 'No, for oxen cannot read.' With the apostle, he was sure that the law was all along meant to teach something higher, and we can see how. If people are to take care of working animals, how much more must they take care of their servants, and how much more must they care for their *spiritual* helpers. What is stated in the law as a binding principle at the lowest level, trains the people to learn and honour that same principle at a higher level, and so Paul is able to conclude – 'Even so hath the Lord ordained that they which preach the gospel should live of the gospel' *(1 Corinthians 9.14)*.

In giving us an example of correct interpretation, Paul does not ask – 'What did Moses literally say? – for that is the limit of the sense,' but he shows that the words had wider significance. There-fore, he tells us that it was never God's purpose solely to safeguard bovine rights, but to proclaim an ethical and spiritual principle applicable ultimately to the church. Calvin also says –

> 'If [the Lord] wants the dumb animals to be treated well, He expects much greater fairness to be shown by men in their dealings with one another. We must not make the mistake of thinking that Paul means to explain the commandment allegori-cally, for some empty-headed creatures make this an excuse for turning everything to allegory, so that they must change dogs into men, trees into angels, and convert the whole of Scripture into an amusing game.'

The point here is that the text is frequently more extensive in meaning than at first appears, and while the *words* and *phrases* must be honoured in their literal meaning, the passage may have a richer purpose. This cannot be summed up by the old adage – 'One mean-ing; many applications' – because applications are thought up by us. They are only the preacher's best endeavours. We must not just think up application, but try first to grasp how much the Holy Spirit is saying in a passage. In this particular case (and the next) the human author, who was Moses, probably did understand the wider meaning himself, but this meaning is not apparent to us if we shut ourselves in to the literal statement.

Another passage illustrating the point is *Deuteronomy 22.10* – 'Thou shalt not plow with an ox and an ass together.' Are we to limit ourselves to the literal sense, or should we believe that this law gives a *principle* and has other associations in mind? Should we not expand it to apply to human and spiritual situations where unmatched people, or unmatched activities are foolishly yoked together as in ecumenical alliances, or the use of pop groups in wor-ship? Paul applies this law to Christian fellowship in *2 Corinthians 6.14* (including compromising with idolaters), and it is frequently applied by preachers to the marriage of a believer with an unbeliever, and other inappropriate associations. The same kind of message appears in the law against wearing a garment of dissimilar textiles *(Deuteronomy 22.11)*.

It is noticeable that the chief stable for the modern approach is the world of the neo-evangelical seminaries, whose professors do not usually care for the doctrine of biblical separation from false teachers, and often welcome worldly methods into church life. They do not want to see modern spiritual battles pre-visioned in the old laws of Israel, or in the narratives. To stick rigidly to examining the text in its historical context as the sole task of the interpreter, brings no challenge to God's people today about the perils around them. Better and sounder evangelicals should note the stable from which modern approach ideas first came into the evangelical world.

And what shall we make of the law of the battlement in *Deuteronomy 22.8*? –

> 'When thou buildest a new house, then thou shalt make a battlement for thy roof, that thou bring not blood upon thine house, if any man fall from thence.'

C. H. Spurgeon shows the way to expound this law, pointing out that God keeps His own law in the doctrine of the perseverance of the saints, and we must do the same in our families, protecting children by godly example and instruction from falling into spiritual disaster. According to Spurgeon, this was the original intention of the passage, and arguably even more important than children sustaining physical injury – but not according to the humanistic straitjacket of the modern approach.

While these 'sundry judicial laws' expired with the passing of the Jewish church-state, their 'general equity' lives on (say the Westminster and Baptist Confessions, among others), meaning that their inherent fairness (especially in spiritual matters) remains, and they must be expounded and applied this way.

We must say a further word on the issue of how much the original

human author understood of his words. He may often have understood his words far better than we realise. He may have grasped the
types of Christ, rejoiced over the evangelical doctrines reflected in
events, and appreciated many of the implicit spiritual lessons. Take
Moses, when he wrote up the event of his giving the covenant in the
land of Moab *(Deuteronomy 29-30)*. When Paul quotes his words in
Romans 10.6-10, he implies that Moses knew that he was speaking
Gospel language. Paul begins the quotation with the fascinating
words – 'But the righteousness which is of faith speaketh on this
wise . . .'

Is Paul saying that Moses understood his words to be about justification by faith, or is Paul saying that the Gospel was secretly
speaking *in* the words of Moses? We think probably the former.
Either way, modern approach interpreters do not expect Gospel
doctrine from Moses, but because we let our *Romans* quotation
show us the way, we do. Their quest to remain within the human
author's meaning invariably restricts that meaning to a single surface probability, and we must not imitate them in this.

It is true that once we reject the idea that our *sole* task is to stay
within the original author's obviously intended meaning, there is a
danger we may indulge in wildly imaginative interpretations, but
not if exposition is restrained and guided by the principles of interpretation we shall look at, all of which happen to be the very
opposite of modern approach errors.

4

The Super-Simplified Bible
Single sense only
(The second defective rule)

WHAT OF the claim that every passage of Scripture has but a single sense or meaning, and no other? The outstanding Puritan William Ames is sometimes quoted as expressing this idea when he wrote: 'There is only one meaning for every place in Scripture.' Is this true? It certainly is, if we mean words or sentences. A *word* will have only one sense in any place, the clear 'dictionary' meaning (or one of the legitimate meanings) of that word. The expositor may well dig to find out the exact intention of the word in a particular context, and any possible nuances, but he must not attach other meanings from mere opinion or personal choice. He must not take, as it were, more than one bite at the word so as to create an additional text.

But the modern approach goes much further than this, strapping the expositor more firmly into his humanistic straitjacket. It is clear they want a single sense not just for every *word* or sentence, but also for every *passage*. However, this is a further undue limitation on Scripture. Modern approach writers claim that this also was the view of the Reformers, but once again they pick up the antagonism of the latter towards the multiple meanings and wild allegories proposed in medieval Rome, and make too much out of it. It was while criticising the 'mere monkey game' of gymnastic interpreters that Luther declared –

> 'The Holy Ghost is the all-simplest writer in Heaven and earth, and so the words can have no more than one and the simplest sense, which we call the scriptural or literal meaning.'

With this we heartily agree, but Luther did not refer to whole passages – only to words and sentences, because he taught that it was essential to study the Old Testament through Christ-seeing lenses, believing that the whole Bible spoke about Christ. (He rejected wild allegorisation and espoused the 'typological interpretation' of the Old Testament, nowadays often called the 'spiritual interpretation'.) So, Luther saw types of Christ, of the church, and parallels with the Christian's spiritual warfare in the Old Testament, not apparent from the literal sense of the passage, but he did not change the literal meaning of words and phrases.

There is yet more to think about on this subject of 'single sense,' because it easily becomes a restriction to 'simple sense'. If a major government issues a statement on some aspect of foreign policy, other nations analyse it very closely to see what is implied for a variety of possible situations. The document will have a general drift, but built into it will be indications of the thinking of the issuing government in a number of directions. If God issues a communiqué we dare not read it as though it were a book of rules for primary schoolchildren, but this is what the modern approach tends to do. While demanding the most complex analytical processes, they expect only one single (and usually ultra-simple) meaning in any passage.

When we study a passage of Scripture, we look at the overall subject and the main themes, but then we look carefully for the subordinate matters that appear. If God gives, for example, a reason why we should obey a particular duty, that reason may be taken by itself as worthy of study and application. In the epistles there are main points, supporting arguments, counsels for implementation, encouragements and warnings, and all are God's profound utterances. Without creating a multiplicity of meanings for words, there is an important and life-giving variety of topics nestling under the main theme, and these are of great importance to us, and must edify. But all tend to be vanquished by the exaggerated notion of single sense.

When we study a passage we seek first to identify the main topic – and how brilliantly Calvin does this in his commentaries on the epistles, chasing the themes through the pages. Then we methodically list all the sub-themes, issues, and observations, not to mention the illustrations, and we notice that some of these are so significant they could be profitably studied as stand-alone principles. And sometimes, by noting these seemingly secondary matters in a text, we are even forced to change our mind and elevate a 'subordinate' matter to first place and so revise our opinion about what the main theme is. Furthermore, a gem of devotional comfort may sit in a grand statement of doctrine, or vice versa. We must never allow 'single sense' to sweep away the riches of the Word.

The overstretched idea of single sense ruins entire Bible books, as in the case of *Jeremiah*, where modern approach commentators are so locked into the view that the prophet is making a 'political' appeal to the nation, that they miss his fervent soul-winning appeals to individual souls – some of the richest and most stirring pieces of evangelistic reasoning in the Bible.

The *Book of Genesis* contains all the so-called doctrines of grace, and this is clearly one of its main purposes, but to see them the expositor must look with New Testament eyes (as Paul urges). Superimposed on the narratives there is many an overshadowing doctrine which must be deduced (and which may or may not have been apparent to the human author). It is literal history, but it also shows God's outworking of election and grace in action.

5

The Blind-Date Bible

No presuppositions or expectations
(The third defective rule)

THIS THIRD feature of the modern approach insists that the interpreter must not bring to a passage any religious opinions, expectations or presuppositions about its meaning. If he does he will be guilty of the heinous crime of eisegesis, which is reading *into* the text what you want it to mean. He must not know anything about the text he is going to meet. This is extremely intimidating to those starting out on the road of exposition. Evacuate from your mind, this formidable rule commands, all the instincts of a large-hearted preacher in search of a spiritual message, and come to the text in a totally dispassionate, objective, 'neutral' way. No preconditions! it thunders. But why? In order that we may honour the first rule, and limit our understanding of the passage to the face-value meaning of the human author. Not all advocates of the modern approach go along with this, but even those who uphold a degree of expectation, limit it quite severely.

The breathtaking daring in this idea is that it sweeps away all that the New Testament explicitly tells us to do, because we have three major texts (plus numerous examples) instructing us to go to the Old Testament with our minds primed, prepared or preconditioned to expect certain things. We are provided with a detailed 'interpretive grid', to be placed over every Old Testament passage in order to identify the doctrines and pastoral messages which the Holy Spirit has placed there. This list of presuppositions and pastoral expectations is the very hermeneutic provided by the Lord, but the modern approach seems to loathe it.

We may think of the work of a physician examining a patient to make a diagnosis. His mind is well stocked with the causes for each group of symptoms, and he will deftly eliminate first one possibility, then another as he moves to a conclusion. If he brings to the process absolutely no memory store of possibilities, and no expectations, he will be entirely dependent on instrumental and laboratory tests, and he will hardly know which to select. Similarly the preacher must approach a passage with some idea of what he is to look for, but the range of possibilities must be provided by the Bible. We turn, therefore, to the three great texts that set out these possibilities – our 'interpretive grid'.

Expectations prescribed in Romans 15.4

'For whatsoever things were written aforetime were written for our learning, that we through patience and comfort of the scriptures might have hope.'

Romans 15.4, referred to earlier, gives emphatic assurance that the Old Testament Scriptures were written for the teaching of believers in the Gospel age, building up their patience (endurance and perseverance), their comfort (*paraklesis*, meaning being called to the instructor's side for comfort or for exhortation), and also their hope (or happy anticipation of heavenly glory). We must look to Old Testament passages, says Paul, for these things.

We are to expect such exhortations and encouragements, and so expositors must go to the Old Testament as prospectors for gold, seeking to recognise and mine the significance and lesson-purpose in the record, according to the apostle's great hermeneutical statement. The abolition of expectations insisted on by modern approach teachers obviously prevents this. From *Romans 15.4* we supply to our 'interpretive grid' these items: teaching or doctrines, lessons in endurance and perseverance, subjective comfort and exhortation, and insights into future glory for the believer's anticipation. The next text will add to the list.

Expectations prescribed in 1 Corinthians 10.1-12

'Moreover, brethren, I would not that ye should be ignorant, how that all our fathers were under the cloud, and all passed through the sea; and were all baptized unto Moses in the cloud and in the sea; and did all eat the same spiritual meat; and did all drink the same spiritual drink: for they drank of that spiritual Rock that followed them: and that Rock was Christ. But with many of them God was not well pleased: for they were overthrown in the wilderness. Now these things were our examples, to the intent we should not lust after evil things, as they also lusted ... Neither let us tempt Christ ... Neither murmur ye, as some of them also murmured, and were destroyed of the destroyer. Now all these things happened unto them for ensamples: and they were written for our admonition, upon whom the ends of the world are come. Wherefore let him that thinketh he standeth take heed lest he fall.'

Here the apostle first expresses his desire that expositors (he actually addresses all believers) should not be ignorant of the typical or figurative significance of what happened at the time of the Exodus and the wilderness wanderings, but his words clearly extend to all Old Testament history. As we read, the extent to which Paul associates these events with Christ and the Christian life almost shocks us. He tells preachers to go to these texts with very great expectations. We are to discover in the Exodus, for example, a picture of baptism along with many other figurative parallels to

Christian experience. Paul speaks of how the Israelites' meat indicates spiritual meat, and of how they drank from a 'spiritual Rock' representing Christ. He goes on to relate how their various failings due to disobedience constitute lessons to people living in the present age to seek salvation and holiness.

The sixth verse could not be more plain, saying that all these events were examples (the Greek is *figures*) to regulate our behaviour in a later age, and to sanctify us, and that the expositor-preacher's task is to draw these lessons from the passage. But how can he do so if his mind is not primed to see them, and his expectations are too low?

Many of the events referred to in *1 Corinthians 10* are recorded in *Numbers.* Paul says –

> 'Now all these things happened unto them for ensamples: and they are written for our admonition, upon whom the ends of the world are come' *(1 Corinthians 10.11).*

The old fashioned word *ensamples (KJV)* means more than examples, it means types or patterns, and these are the lessons provided by the Spirit of God to keep Christians from falling (verse 12). The Israelites were a genuine church, and their events more than an empty show, but at the same time they provide pictures for the church of today, and are recorded for that purpose.

From *1 Corinthians 10.1-12,* the apostle's longest lesson in interpretation, we take for our 'grid' the following expectations and presuppositions. We will expect figures (and lessons) of spiritual food and drink; of baptism even, and the Lord's Supper; of Christ the Rock; of moral and spiritual discipline; of idolatry, hypocrisy and adultery (spiritual adultery is clearly in view); of discontent and doubting; of falling short of salvation; and of backsliding. We will seek to recognise God's intended *ensamples* or patterns (in people and events) to stir the believer's sanctification and hope in Christ. (Of course, these will also be relevant for evangelistic sermons.)

Expectations prescribed in 2 Timothy 3.16-17

'All scripture is given by inspiration of God, and is profitable for doctrine, for reproof, for correction, for instruction in righteousness: that the man of God may be perfect, throughly furnished unto all good works.'

Discussion of such a well-known text is hardly needed, except to say that it is more than an observation about Timothy's past, but an authoritative announcement that all Scripture (the Old Testament is in mind from verse 15) is to be regarded as a source of instruction for application to the Christian life and walk, and that this was always God's intention. Why, then, should this be banned as an expectation or presupposition in the interpreter's mind? Surely it is commanded.

Paul says that in order that the believer may be fully equipped for holiness and service, the Scriptures are designed to yield up doctrine, reproof, correction (when drifting off course), helps, warnings and encouragements to sanctification. Such lessons are the purpose of the inspired Word and are infinitely more important than Jewish history and Holy Land background information.

Our 'interpretive grid' is forming, but it is not quite complete, because other expectations are given to us in various New Testament quotations from the Old, which provide examples of how the Old is to be used. Taking the topics already listed, we logically expand and augment them (from New Testament quotations) to form the following list. This will complete the 'grid' to be, as it were, placed over any Old Testament passage. We ask – Does the passage contain or reflect any or several of the following topics? (First, we list again the topics derived from the three texts.) Lessons in endurance and perseverance; comfort and exhortation; insights of future glory; figures and types of spiritual food; ordinances of Christ; pictures of (spiritual) idolatry, hypocrisy, adultery, discontent and doubting; the folly of remaining unsaved or backsliding; reproof, correction, warnings and encouragements; lessons, counsels and examples for ongoing sanctification.

Now, we tidy up the list, logically expanding the topics above, and adding some which New Testament quotations show are also in the Old Testament.

- **The being and character of God**
- **The person and work of Christ either in types or verbal prophecies**
- **The doctrine of redemption and the terms and way of salvation**
- **The Gospel**
- **Evangelistic, persuasive arguments**
- **The plan and purpose of God**
- **The fall and depravity of human nature**
- **Broader insights into human nature**
- **Saving faith**
- **The believer's faith**
- **Spiritual food and strength**
- **God's covenants, the doctrines of grace**
- **True and false worship**
- **The future church of Christ, its membership and order**
- **Backsliding and recovery**
- **Witness and service, right and wrong methods in the Lord's service**
- **Prayer**
- **Advance in holiness**
- **Promises**
- **Warnings**

It is a good idea to keep a list of such topics in one's Bible, but the regular preacher will soon carry these themes in his head, as a physician carries his knowledge of symptoms and possible illnesses. Is such a preacher not vulnerable to reading these topics into the passage of Scripture being studied? Not if he is robustly honest and careful. If he is fit to be a preacher, he will surely take care not to foist a subject on to the text. We do not need an entirely new, man-made system of interpretation (destroying the nature of Scripture in the process) to replace the duty of honest, sane diligence on the part of an expositor.

6

The Fragmented Bible
No subsequent text or doctrine may be used to explain a passage
(The fourth defective rule)

O REMIND readers of this painfully secular, modern rule of interpretation, it says that no biblical doctrine or other text may be allowed to throw light on a passage unless it was known to the original human author. This rule destroys the chief maxim of interpretation spelt out in the great seventeenth-century confessions (and, of course, in the Bible). The Westminster and Baptist (1689) Confessions both declare:

> 'The infallible rule of interpretation of Scripture is the Scripture itself; and therefore when there is a question about the true and full sense of any Scripture (which is not manifold, but one), it must be searched by other places that speak more clearly.'

The Confession writers, representing the mainstream Reformation tradition, knew nothing of using only prior revelation to explain a passage. The Bible is but one book, say the Confessions, by which they mean that it was entirely written by God at the same 'time' in eternity past, and therefore it must not be viewed as the product of a multiplicity of authors, the early ones having no idea what the later ones would say. God certainly inspired many authors, but the material is His own.

We shall see later in this book how disastrous it is to attempt a study of *Judges* without paying heed to the instructions of *Hebrews 11*, assuring us of the character, faith and spiritual objectives of the heroes of that era. Ignoring this, the modern approach commentators (and there are many) turn individual judges into faithless and often immoral rogues, so that the meaning of the book becomes the opposite of what the Lord intended. Modern approach teachers say we must interpret as though we were secularists or theological liberals, pretending that *Judges* was not written by God, but by a mere man who knew nothing of *Hebrews*. The latter must, therefore, not influence our quest for the human author's intended meaning. In fact, we would say that the integrity and spirituality of the judges is plain from the narrative (as we show later) but the comments in *Hebrews* confirm that view.

The Confession writers also spoke of 'the consent of all the parts' of the Bible, referring to its perfectly consistent nature. Any text may throw light on any other text, whether before or after it, if it addresses the same subject. Out of the Reformation came an understanding called the analogy of faith,* which very broadly speaks of how every correct understanding of a text in the Bible will agree with the chief doctrines drawn from passages clearly dealing with the same subject.

In other words, the Bible will itself, through its unmistakeable

---

*A term coined by a church father, but given a new meaning at the Reformation. This principle is generally based on *1 Corinthians 2.13* and *2 Timothy 1.13* (where Paul speaks of the 'form' or pattern or outline sketch of sound words which should always be held fast); and *Acts 15.7* and *14-15* where James unites Peter's revelation about Gentile conversion with that of the prophet Amos.

chief doctrines, act as judge of our interpretations. So we gather together the chief doctrines of the faith that are spelled out so plainly, usually in many places, secure in the knowledge that because the parts of the Bible always agree, these will never be contradicted. These certain Bible doctrines may then be used to test our understanding of other texts. This is one of the most important rules of traditional evangelical interpretation.

Returning to the ban on using later texts to interpret earlier ones, we think of the *Book of Leviticus* and the necessity of New Testament light to really bring it to life for Christian use. A notable nineteenth-century writer, Andrew Jukes, demonstrates the power of such an approach in his slim but rich book – *The Law of the Offerings.** By uniting the clear light of Calvary with the typical offerings, the latter are seen to say even more than the Gospels and *Romans* about the full nature and glory of Christ's work, and there is remarkable stimulation for a sanctified life. There is no other way of preaching *Leviticus*, as all the great preachers in print on this book have shown.

One of the greatest sermons in history was the so-called 'deathless sermon' preached by William Carey at Nottingham in May 1792, the message that lit the torch for the modern missionary movement. The text was *Isaiah 54* about the desolate woman who is to enlarge the place of her tent, and stretch forth the curtains of her habitation to receive a great number of Gentile children. From this passage Carey proved the necessity of missionary labours and human instrumentality, but according to many advocates of the modern approach his sermon should never have been preached from that text, because the literal wording of the chapter does not specifically identify the work of the New Testament church.

What entitled Carey to make it a prophecy of the church age?

---

*The Law of the Offerings: The Five Tabernacle Offerings and Their Spiritual Significance, Andrew Jukes, Kregel, 1966.

He saw it in *Galatians 4.27-28*, where Paul quotes the opening of Isaiah's wonderful words and declares to his converted Gentile readers, 'Now we, brethren, as Isaac was, are the children of promise.' With this in mind Carey noticed that *Isaiah 54* followed *Isaiah 53*, and what could be more natural than that Pentecost and the church age should follow Calvary? (Or that the Gospel offer of *Isaiah 55* should follow both?) By the modern approach, however, as propounded by many, the Christian church would lose one of the most sublime chapters of promise in the Bible, because the interpreter must never let a later text throw light on an earlier one.

The idea that only antecedent (or prior) scriptures must be allowed to influence our understanding of a passage is yet another indication of the secular humanism inherent in the modern approach, present to an extent which makes it virtually a confession of unbelief, deserving no place in the thinking of preachers of the eternal, divine Word.

7

The Strictly-Scientific Bible
No allegorising or spiritualising
(The fifth defective rule)

THE INTERPRETER-PREACHER, they tell us, must never allegorise or spiritualise a passage, for this is utterly reprehensible, abominable and unthinkable (words used by some of the teachers of the modern approach). Is it always wrong to say that something in the Bible stands for something else? Are the powerful scare-words of these teachers justified?

We recognise that unwarranted and even foolish allegorisation does take place, and we appreciate the consternation of many seminary educators. But to claim there are no allegories in the Bible, and no passages which are meant to be 'spiritualised' is a very extreme position which simply fails to honour the range of literary styles in the Bible. It also frightens preachers away from drawing legitimate parallels for today, a practice which follows the text closely, but sees modern spiritual situations reflected there. The total ban on allegorising or spiritualising (by which *we* mean – drawing parallels) is a choice case of administering poison to cure a fever, or indiscriminately spraying systemic weedkiller over a bed of roses to curb unwanted weeds. Of course absurdly misplaced allegorisation goes on, but the remedy is not a Draconian ban, because the Bible undoubtedly contains *some* allegories, *more* types, *even more* parables, *many* symbols and *countless* parallels. It is a serious fault of modern approach teachers that they confidently strike out what God has written.

The preacher is certainly not entitled to decide for himself that any narrative is allegory or that it yields a parallel for today. He must use certain rules to determine that it is right for him to proceed on this basis, and the seminary hermeneutics department would be better employed teaching the old rules, not despoiling the prophetic and wisdom literature of their figures.

If we define 'allegory' as a fictional narrative intended to describe something similar or parallel to it (just as Christian's journey in *The Pilgrim's Progress* pictures the believer's spiritual journey), then allegory is very rare in the Bible, but it is there. This writer joins with the overwhelming majority of preachers in church history in identifying *Song of Solomon* as an allegorical book speaking of the mutual love of Christ and His people. The arguments for this are weighty and powerful (and usually neither mentioned nor faced by writers contending for a contrary view).[*]

There is even more 'allegorical' material in the Bible, for the lengthier parables in *Proverbs* may strictly be classified as such, although we prefer to call them parables. Many passages in *Proverbs* are unmistakeable allegories, or parables, as the title of the book proclaims, for the Hebrew word translated as *Proverbs* literally means parables or comparisons. To preach only on literal adultery from *Proverbs 7* would be a great shame, when Solomon tells us that in this part of the book he is appealing to the naive to find deep

---

[*]See *The Mutual Love of Christ and His People*, Peter Masters, Wakeman Trust, 2004.

understanding, subtlety and discretion, clearly pointing to that spiritual light gloriously described in the wisdom chapters. As the title of the book implies, the story of the adulteress is a parable, and once the interpreter sees this, he derives compressed and powerful evangelistic reasoning from it.

To summarise this point, there is, firstly, allegorical material in the Bible, although it is rare. Secondly, there are many parables in both the Old and the New Testament. Thirdly, there are types to be recognised and expounded in the Old Testament (to be referred to again shortly). Fourthly, there are symbols and symbolic language, particularly in the prophetic books, and also in *Psalms*.

Fifthly, there are very many passages in the Old Testament which are literal history, and yet must be 'spiritualised'. To spiritualise is to see that historic events in the Bible have a lesson, for they chronicle the behaviour of believers and unbelievers in relation to God's requirements. These are recorded because they reflect our lives today, so that we may learn lessons of faith and commitment, and see God's ways toward people. They are events which *parallel* the experience of Gospel age believers, and God intended them to do this when they were put in the Old Testament record.

We may spiritualise (in this sense) in evangelistic preaching, because Israel often serves as a 'type' of humanity in general. The favoured Israelites were a 'sample' of all human beings, who receive great privileges (being higher than the animals and endowed with special faculties and powers), and who receive many demonstrations of the power of God (in creation and human complexity, for example). What Israel did with her privileges and how God responded to her (sometimes with great grace) has application to the whole world. Unbelief is illustrated, the attitudes of fallen hearts to the living God are exposed, and His remonstrations with people are seen. Here are many detailed challenges and insights into God's grace for utilisation by preachers in evangelism.

We may also 'spiritualise' passages of Bible history in application to believers, because Israel also mirrors the church of Christ. At no point do we deny the history or turn it into allegory, but we note the parallels and draw the obvious lessons for today (seeing them all the more clearly because our minds are crammed with the expectations of the topic-list or grid outlined earlier). If the seminary student understands the prohibition of spiritualising to forbid the use of Scripture as just described, he will be unable to minister with real purpose and spiritual blessing from the Old Testament.

As far as Old Testament Israel is concerned, the author, incidentally, believes that while she sometimes mirrors the church and sometimes all people, she never represents the United States or Britain or any other specific nation, as though there were on earth a special Gentile nation.

How shall we guard against unwarranted and irresponsible interpretation? Certainly not by blanket prohibitions and scare-words. In the past, this has always been recognised as a very sensitive matter. In addressing his students, C. H. Spurgeon would prescribe no more than the use of care and common sense, although he warmly commended the rules of Patrick Fairbairn (1805-1874), a Scottish preacher and theologian and author of *The Typology of Scripture*, *The Interpretation of Prophecy* and other great works. Despite some debatable areas, Fairbairn's rules for identifying and handling types are still unsurpassed in our opinion.[*]

The kind of spiritualising outlined here – no more than spiritual application of the passage – is very, very different from the so-called 'principlization' or 'principlizing' proposed by leading contenders for the modern approach. This assumes that a passage has been exegeted strictly in accordance with modern approach rules, then

---

[*]See *The Typology of Scripture*, Patrick Fairbairn, Kregel, 1989, and *The Interpretation of Prophecy*, Patrick Fairbairn, Banner of Truth, 1993.

(at the very end of the process) the expounder seeks to make an application. We contend, however, that an expounder working by the biblical rules looks for the purpose and application from the very beginning of the process, using the apostle's presuppositions and expectations. (Principlization is critiqued a few pages hence.)

The interpreting of symbols in prophetic books is well monitored by the rule of consistency, a rather general standard which assumes that symbols have much the same meaning throughout the Bible, so that the symbolic use of 'mountain' may be expected to have the same meaning in every place. This may not always be correct, but it is good enough to form a safe restriction on an interpreter's bounding imagination. We should also expect a figure or symbol to be reasonably obvious in meaning.

Old Testament types are best identified by their being referred to as typical in the New Testament (although this is of no help to users of the modern approach, for this holds that no New Testament text shall be allowed to throw light on a passage in the Old). However, there are doubtless types not explicitly mentioned in the New Testament, the prime example being Joseph. He is given more space in *Genesis* than either Abraham or Jacob, and the parallels between his life and that of Christ are numerous and inescapable. Actually, it is highly probable that Joseph is seen in the New Testament as a type, chiefly in the words of the Saviour (quoted earlier) to the two perplexed disciples on the road to Emmaus, following the resurrection:

> 'O fools, and slow of heart to believe all that the prophets have spoken: Ought not Christ to have suffered these things, and to enter into his glory? And beginning at Moses and all the prophets, he expounded unto them in all the scriptures the things concerning himself' *(Luke 24.25-27).*

Evidently the Lord showed from Moses, as well as from the prophets, His death, resurrection and ascension. Paul did the same, being even more specific about the Pentateuch, for he says he preached –

'none other things than those which the prophets *and Moses* did
say should come: that Christ should suffer, and that he should be
the first that should rise from the dead' *(Acts 26.22-23).*

If the Lord (probably) and the apostle Paul (definitely) say Moses
spoke of the resurrection, then he did. But where – if not in the typical history of Joseph? As Dean John Burgon once asked in a series of
stirring questions to literal-sense extremists in his day, 'Where is
Christ in Moses, if not there *[in the life of Joseph]*? Show us!'

Robert S. Candlish, in his classic exposition of *Genesis* represents
the traditional view of Joseph, saying:

'Resemblances of a more or less typical character cannot fail to be
observed between him and Christ . . . we have to recognise a
closer bond of union than that which incidental coincidences
might establish . . . it might almost be said, with literal truth, that
Joseph is the Jesus of the Old Testament church's history.'

Robert Candlish goes on to list remarkable parallels. (1) Joseph's
first appearance in Egypt in a low state; (2) his nobility of nature
being recognised there from the beginning; (3) his manifold and
complex temptation; (4) his suffering, which was worse than death
to him, through his refusal to yield when tempted; (5) his being
owned, even in the lowest depths, as one chosen and beloved of
the Lord. Humiliation and exaltation are both there, in a life so
well known among the Israelites, prefiguring Messiah, and also (by
spiritual application) representative of the Christian young person
standing for the Lord in a hostile world.

The Word of God is nothing less than the Book of God, profound, glorious, and spiritually instructive throughout to the souls
of His people. Never should it be 'secularised' and 'humanised' by
being stripped of its continuous spiritual significance, imagery,
parables, parallels, figures, and even (although rarer) allegories.

8

The Add-on Application Bible
Applying from the text's literal meaning alone
(The sixth defective rule)

THE MODERN approach demands that the application of a passage must be built on the face-value meaning arrived at by applying the mistaken principles of these recent chapters. Supposing we are working on an Old Testament passage, this means we take up the human author's surface meaning, looking for nothing deeper in the words or in the events recorded, seeing only one thought in each sentence, bringing no expectations to the passage, allowing no later text to throw light on it, and recoiling in terror at the possibility of a type, symbol, parable, or spiritual parallel. This restrictive thinking must never leave us, for we are told to stay at all times within the horizons of the original speaker's audience when they first heard his address.

Having shut ourselves into the idea that the Bible is 'like any other book', we are then urged to write out a few bland paragraphs representing exactly what the text says. Last of all we are to compose the application for today's hearers by a method named by one leading advocate of the modern approach – 'principlization'. The problem is that by this stage we are firmly straitjacketed, our minds having had no scope to think in terms of God's intended message, and the pastoral possibilities.

Some modern approach books propose the following procedure for constructing an application. By a little more technical probing of words we are to examine the 'paragraphs' of the passage to see if there are similar phrases, questions, pivotal words, repeated words, or any special emphasis on which we may build clever-looking headings for a sermon. It all seems rather tame after the excessively complex stages of analysis. To put the meat on these headings is then up to us. All that exegetical work has only given us a subject, or a series of points. It is sometimes difficult to see much difference between this and the preparation of a topical sermon, except that in the latter case the preacher thinks of his own topic.

The material to be preached under the headings will owe little to the text (because parallels and implications are not approved of), and so it must come out of the preacher's head. The old approach is so different, for it continually makes use of the whole passage, drawing parallels to show needs, sins, acts of faith, proving of the Lord, comforts and exhortations. The modern approach is not true expository preaching at all.

Looking at the examples of sermon outlines provided by advocates of the modern approach in their books, the results are on the whole woeful, lacking any substantial spiritual help, strength, or comfort derived from the passage. The tag-on idea of principlization is a desperate rummaging in the text for snappy heading possibilities, carried out by a mind that expects nothing about Christ or the church or eternity or the inner spiritual warfare of a Christian. Paul tells us that God is writing about *these* things, but for such an expositor they are out of sight. (How plainly this is to be seen in so many modern commentaries which give not a clue about the *message* of the passage.)

In the event, this writer finds himself disagreeing profoundly with every sample outline the modern approach teachers provide, because they always miss the built-in spiritual purpose of the passage. Some of the sermon outlines we refer to are by brilliant men, but shackled by the rules of the modern approach even they achieve very little.

Space and courtesy prevent us from reproducing the examples provided in books presenting the modern approach, but they always miss the point, because there is no *spiritual life* context in the mind of the expositor; no distinctively *Christian* context; no *soul-reaching* context; no *church* context; no *doctrine-imparting* context; and no *worship and service* context. These (and more) are the *eyes* essential for seeing why the record is there, and what it means.

We have just mentioned doctrine-imparting context, but, of course, these teachers believe very strongly in such a strictly progressive development of doctrine in the Bible that to bring New Testament eyes to an Old Testament passage would be inappropriate. What hope is there of seeing great doctrines reflected in the early portions of the Bible? We must make ourselves forget that it is all written by God.

We have surely said enough to show that these ideas, widespread as they may be, are miles away from the interpretive method of the Bible and of the great tradition of past Bible preachers. The modern approach dismisses the belief that the Bible provides definite rules and steps of its own. It prevents expositors from exercising their Christ-honouring, pastoral, fervently evangelical sensitivities, so vital to understanding and preaching the Word.

Every one of these six 'principles' undergirding and permeating the stages of interpretation advocated by the modern approach is disastrously misconceived. Followers of the *old* approach should certainly honour scrupulously the plain sense of a passage, scrutinise context, carefully observe the situation of the writer and people of the time, identify the type of book, make sure they properly understand the words, and allow a sound 'analogy of faith' to monitor their conclusions. But from the beginning they will have before their minds evangelical doctrine, Christ, today's church (and the forces ranged against it), in order to discern the reason why the original record was preserved in the Word. They will be open to types and pastoral parallels.

For preachers trained in today's undermining procedures, who wish to be delivered from its long-term effects, we recommend older, applied commentaries by men who immersed themselves in the whole Bible as one book, seeing all from a New Testament perspective, believing it to be God's message for His people in every age, and interpreting Scripture by Scripture. The reading of Hall's *Contemplations* for historical portions of the Old Testament, and Matthew Henry's *Commentary* (despite its smattering of idiosyncrasies) will do much to heal the detached, unapplied spirit of the modern approach, but, of course, there are many other great works that may be used. Such books open a new world to those who have fallen prey to the 'wholly human Bible', bringing narratives and discourses from flat monochrome into three-dimensional colour. Small wonder the sermons of past generations continue to sell in great quantities, while sermons of the last thirty years remain unpublished.

9

What the Reformers Really Said
Calvin on types and parallels

Before the Reformation it was fashionable for clergy to assume that there were various 'levels' of meaning (usually four) to be mined out of every passage of Scripture. Mystical and fanciful allegorical methods of interpretation were well entrenched. Even Augustine, who taught that the literal sense of the Scripture should be seen as paramount, accepted the idea that a passage will have several levels of sense.

In such a context, it is not surprising that the Reformers strongly emphasised the great and primary importance of the literal, plain sense of the text. However, in several books by modern approach authors, Calvin (as well as Luther) is carried to an extreme to support their ideas, being quoted as saying that the original author's intended surface meaning is the *sole* correct meaning of the text. Modern approach authors triumphantly parade words from Calvin's letter of dedication in his commentary on *Romans*:

> 'Since it is almost his *[the interpreter's]* only task to unfold the mind of the writer whom he has undertaken to expound, he

misses his mark, or at least strays outside his limits, by the extent to which he leads his readers away from the meaning of his author.'

Is Calvin here supporting the theory of the modern approach school? He is not, for here lies a most valuable feature of Calvin's method of interpretation, long discussed by Calvin scholars. On the one hand, he repeatedly stresses the need to cling closely to the human author's intention, while on the other he also insists on seeing the intention of the Holy Spirit, and what He intended to say to the church. Noted Calvin scholars speak of how he pursues the intention of the Holy Spirit within the literal sense, viewed with spiritual eyes, to find Christ and His church in the Old Testament.

One may see Calvin's balanced position in his introduction to *Isaiah*, where he asserts that ultimately the text contains no *human* reasoning, but only the revelation given by the Spirit of God.

Professor Brevard Childs of Yale Divinity School in his recent work on *Isaiah*[*] summarises Calvin's method in these words:

'Because the Bible is a written text of a human author, its words can be studied grammatically as any other writing. However, this is only part of the task; the relation between the human and divine nature of Scripture requires a much more subtle approach . . . It is crucial to understand that what Calvin means by a text's literal sense is not simply identified with its verbal or historically reconstructed meaning . . . For Calvin, there is . . . a strong force exerted to extend the meaning by adapting the biblical text to the present usage of the church. This bridge or act of application is by the means of a transference, that is, an anagoge [a literary analogy].'

Calvin justly denied that he used allegorisation in the medieval sense, for he did not twist the literal sense of the passage, but made

---

[*]*The Struggle to Understand* ISAIAH *as Christian Scripture*, Brevard S. Childs, Eerdmans, 2004, pp. 207-229.

the passage analogous to the experience of the church, taking his cue from New Testament statements that the Old was written for all ages. He, therefore, read the Old Testament through the eyes of New Testament doctrines, believing, as we have noted, that it is about Christ and His church. In all this, he never strayed from the meaning of the Old Testament passage, but unquestionably extended the sense.

We should allow Calvin to speak for himself. In his commentary on *Galatians* he makes the following superb statement about the plain sense and how it relates to the presence of figures and parallels in the Old Testament. (Needless to say the modern approach writers do not quote this.) Here is the perfect expression of the matter. First, Calvin upholds the literal sense, condemning those who make allegories out of texts at whim; but then he shows that there are parallels between Old Testament events and the church age, and these must be seen and correctly handled. (This comment is on *Galatians 4.24.*) We urge our readers to persevere with this slightly complex quotation as it decisively lays to rest the idea that Calvin was in line with today's modern approach.

> 'For many centuries no man was thought clever who lacked the cunning and daring to transfigure with subtlety the sacred Word of God. This was undoubtedly a trick of Satan to impair the authority of Scripture and remove any benefit out of the reading of it . . . Scripture, they say, is fertile and thus bears multiple meanings. I acknowledge that Scripture is the most rich and inexhaustible fount of all wisdom. But I deny that its fertility consists in the various meanings which anyone may fasten to it at his pleasure. Let us know, then, that the true meaning of Scripture is the natural and simple one, and let us embrace and hold it resolutely. Let us not merely neglect as doubtful, but boldly set aside as deadly corruptions, those pretended expositions which lead us away from literal sense.
>
> 'But what shall we reply to Paul's assertion *[that Abraham's family is an allegory]*? He certainly does not mean that Moses

purposely wrote the story so that it might be turned into an allegory, but is pointing out in what way the story relates to the
present case; that is, when we see there the image of the church
figuratively delineated. And an anagoge [a spiritual, allegorical
interpretation] of this sort is not foreign to the genuine and literal
meaning, when a comparison was drawn between the church and
the family of Abraham. For as the house of Abraham was then the
true church, so it is beyond doubt that the principal and most
memorable events that happened in it are types for us.'

That last statement declares the true position of the Reformer and
all who follow him, and is the position we seek to lay out in this
book, namely that parallels were intended by God.

Earlier in this book we accused the modern approach authors of
selectively quoting Calvin, and what follows is a particularly bad
example. Immediately after the words shown earlier from his commentary on *Romans*, he makes the following statement. Modern
approach writers do not quote this because it destroys their prohibition of the use of later scriptures to explain a text.

'If we understand this epistle *[Romans]* we have a channel opened
up for us to the understanding of the whole of Scripture.'

In other words, Calvin believed that *Romans* should condition and
mould our understanding of all other parts of Scripture, even opening up for us, for example, the *Book of Genesis*. God's intended
spiritual or typical message, which may not be immediately apparent to us, springs to life by the help of *Romans*.

Right and wrong spiritualising

So important is the subject of God's intended figures and parallels
in the Old Testament, that a few further comments on parallels are
provided in the following pages (with a little repetition) to clarify
the position. The vehement tirade against allegorisation mounted by
modern approach books prompts the question – are there allegories

in the Bible? Remember that an allegory is a fictional story used to describe another subject, perhaps a moral message, by suggestive resemblances. It is an extended metaphor, or a moral story. By this definition there are few allegories in the Bible, but there are some, and we have named *Song of Solomon* and the longer 'parables' in the *Book of Proverbs* as examples.

However, when modern approach writers condemn allegorisation, they include in this the drawing of parallels. Yet there are thousands of parallels between things recorded in the Old Testament and the life of the church today, for God has written and preserved the history of the Jews to teach the church how He deals with His people spiritually. When modern approach teachers call allegorisation reprehensible and abominable, they ban all these parallels also, tearing out of the Old Testament its greatest pastoral purpose. This is no way to cure preachers who allegorise the Old Testament out of their imagination. They need to be shown how to correctly recognise and apply pastoral parallels without distorting the text.

Does a preacher have the freedom to choose for himself what an Old Testament narrative represents or parallels? He does not have such liberty. He should not, for example, take the account of David and Goliath and draw from it a sermon about 'the giants in your life' and how they must be slain, specifying a list of sins or objects of covetous desire, or similar ideas. This is merely low-level ingenuity, exploiting the text for sermon points, and failing to do justice to the whole event. This would be wrong 'allegorising' (which oddly enough comes in this case from the sermon notes of a modern approach supporter).

The preacher's imagination spotted a vaguely plausible, but rather trivial connection and failed to notice that the giant was not an obstacle in David's life, but in Israel's. Had he remained faithful to the grammatical sense, he would also have respected that there was only one giant, and no parallel for plural giants in your life.

However, from the beginning of his sermon preparation, the preacher must be aware that the narrative has a purpose, and in this passage the purpose is clearly to provide an example of faith in spiritual warfare and service. What the arm of flesh could not do, God could do through the instrumentality of a faithful man, however young and obscure. The key words say that 'the Lord saveth not with sword and spear: for the battle is the Lord's.' Truly significant parallels abound, such as David's rejection of Saul's armour, surely applicable in principle to such matters as the necessary rejection of the polluted musical idiom and instruments of the world in the battle for souls, or the rejection of most of the fleshly methods and innovations presented in church-growth books. Equally, there are great positive and encouraging lessons to be drawn from the vindication of David's obedience and faith.

The point is that such narratives contain many principles of the spiritual life, of mission, of God's ways, of the rewards of faith, of the consequences of absence of faith and of placing trust in human devices or false doctrine, and these must be drawn out. The pastoral eye must be active from the beginning of preparation, but great care must be exercised to ensure that the parallels drawn are logical, reasonably obvious, worthy, not far-fetched, nor strained, and not concerned merely with minor or trivial matters.

The rule is not hard to follow. In the historical narratives of the Bible, the family of Abraham or the church of the Jewish era represents and illustrates God's dealings with His people in later times. Do we honour these parallels in making faithful spiritual observations and explaining the lessons of faith?

10

Are All Parables and Miracles Gracious?
Do they all present the Gospel message?

WHILE VERY many preachers still regard the parables of Christ as pictures of how to be saved, most modern evangelical Bible dictionaries and commentaries, and strangely, many seminary lecturers, now think they are largely moral lessons, and, sadly, this view is being successfully implanted in a new generation of preachers. However, it is deeply mistaken and out of line with the outlook of Bible believers through most of the history of the church.

The modern approach, with its exaggerated fear of allegories and parables, permits only a minimal point or two from any parable, and frequently sees no Gospel element. If such an element is recognised, it never extends to a full unfolding of the way of salvation. The modern textbooks all say there is no catch-all rule for the interpretation of our Lord's parables, but the old view says there is, and it is the presentation of grace and conversion. Salvation is always there. It is therefore important that we should prove from Scripture that all the parables are designed to be pictures of grace at work, supplying to preachers numerous powerful arguments for reaching all sorts and conditions of lost people.

In *John 16.25* the Saviour says: 'These things have I spoken unto you in proverbs *[literally parables]*: but the time cometh, when I shall no more speak unto you in proverbs, but I shall shew you plainly of the Father.' The Lord intended that to a large extent His parables would obscure His teaching. With a little explanation, such as He gave to His disciples, they would bring to light the way of salvation in a remarkable way, but left unexplained, they could equally veil the truth. This was the Lord's necessary purpose, partly to conceal the way of salvation from those who despised it, partly to prevent murderous violence against Himself (not to mention the disciples) prior to Calvary, and partly (according to *John 16.25*) because the full light of the parables would not dawn until the time of His death and resurrection. There was a 'fuse' in the parables, a delayed-action sense which would be activated by the Saviour's atoning work.

A parable is an analogy from common experience, or a short story illustrating a spiritual truth. The simplest definition says that it is an earthly story with a heavenly meaning, or a salvation lesson. Our Lord's parables are most engaging even when not spiritually understood, but with explanation, they make the truth easy to grasp.

The unvarying heart of every parable is the way of salvation, or entry to the kingdom, as the Lord made clear when explaining the parable of the sower. In *Mark 4.11-12* we read:

> 'Unto you it is given to know the mystery of the kingdom of God: but unto them that are without, all these things are done in parables: that seeing they may see, and not perceive; and hearing they may hear, and not understand; lest at any time they should be converted, and their sins should be forgiven them.'

Clearly, a merely moral message would not have needed veiling, because it would not have lead to conviction and repentance, but the veiling attached to parables shows that they contained the message of salvation.

Furthermore the Lord states clearly that parables convey 'the mystery of the kingdom' and we know that this refers to Christ's kingdom and how it is entered. It refers to the Gospel. Paul uses a similar term 'the mystery of Christ' in *Ephesians 3* to describe the secret hidden from former ages about how the Gentiles would be saved by the Gospel. In *Ephesians 6* he calls it plainly 'the mystery of the gospel'. When, therefore, the Saviour calls His parables vehicles of 'the mystery of the kingdom' He means that they all speak about the way of salvation.

This 'mystery' or 'secret' terminology also occurs in *Matthew 13.34-35* where we read:

> 'All these things spake Jesus unto the multitude in parables; and without a parable spake he not unto them: that it might be fulfilled which was spoken by the prophet, saying, I will open my mouth in parables; I will utter things which have been kept secret from the foundation of the world.'

In other words it was prophesied (by the psalmist in *Psalm 78*) that Messiah would teach in parables, and these would be about the way of salvation.

In *Mark 1.14-15* it is recorded:

> 'Now after that John was put in prison, Jesus came into Galilee, preaching the gospel of the kingdom of God, and saying, The time is fulfilled, and the kingdom of God is at hand: repent ye, and believe the gospel.'

Parables are not specifically mentioned in this verse, but the Lord's entire ministry is here summed up by the word 'gospel', and as parables were the principal element of His ministry, they must be gracious. Parables were uniquely associated with the Lord, there being no others in the New Testament, and as they formed such a special, dominant and memorable part of His teaching, it is unthinkable that they did not proclaim the purpose of His work – the Gospel. They clearly have soul-saving significance, and should not be turned into moral lessons only, but interpreted so as to draw out the way of salvation.

The Saviour taught His disciples how to interpret two of His parables, both of them being obvious salvation messages, and His explanations are decisive in proving that all parables convey the Gospel. The Lord questioned the disciples about the parable of the sower, saying, 'Know ye not this parable? and *how then will ye know all parables?' (Mark 4.13.)* If the disciples knew how to handle one parable, they would know how to handle the others; if they learned to see grace in one, they would see it in all. If, however, some of the parables contained a saving message, while others had a moral message, then the parable of the sower would not have been an ideal pattern for the interpretation of all.

The parallel passage in *Luke 8* provides (in verse 12) a clear identification of salvation issues in the parable, the Lord saying – 'Those by the way side are they that hear; then cometh the devil, and taketh away the word out of their hearts, lest they should believe and be saved.'

The other example of the Saviour teaching the disciples how to interpret a parable is in *Matthew 13.24-43,* where the parable of the wheat and the tares is unfolded. 'Declare unto us the parable of the tares of the field,' they ask, and the explanation is given entirely in terms of salvation and eternal destiny. 'The field is the world; the good seed are the children of the kingdom; but the tares are the children of the wicked one; the enemy that sowed them is the devil; the harvest is the end of the world; and the reapers are the angels.'

Most of the parables of Christ focus on the last judgement and the harvest of souls, and this is all compounded under the term (in *Matthew 13.19*) 'the word of the kingdom'. These, of course, are Gospel themes. *Kingdom, Gospel, faith* and *saved* are wonderfully symphonious terms, spoken of in the parables, and joined with *repent* and *believe*.

However, modern writers will not have it, and it is very sad that commentators who we so often appreciate for their technical exegesis cannot find an evangelistic purpose in the parables. If we have access to older works and published sermons, we receive help in abundance. If we have Spurgeon on parables and miracles, we possess a rich supply of evangelistic application. Indeed, if we have almost any treatment of parables from bygone preachers, we will find the reformed position was 'all Gospel', but for the 'moderns', the lost sheep is about the Father's love, and not specifically about the mechanics of salvation, and the lost coin and the lost son go the same way, the latter being an appeal to the Pharisees to be reasonable. There is no Gospel.

In modern works the parable of the pounds in *Luke 19* is about equal rewards in service, and loss for those who are unfaithful to the Lord, so the parable is virtually reduced to works. The friend at midnight, according to modern approach commentaries, simply means – 'keep praying!' There is nothing more. The rich fool is only a moral lesson about greed. Good men consistently wreck the parables and do not seem to be aware of what they are doing.

Some commentaries are quite bizarre in their failure to see 'the mystery of the kingdom' or 'the gospel' in these parables. An eminent and no doubt godly evangelical in the US, a seminary professor, issued a few years ago an enormous two-volume commentary on *Luke*, this being enthusiastically reviewed by evangelical journals as showing acute power in application. But when we look at the comments on parables, there is practically no salvation in sight, and the pages of scholarly observation become useless. The modern approach has accomplished something liberal theologians never managed to do; it has effectively buried the parables.

Looking for the gracious element in a parable requires a simplified interpretive grid of the kind referred to earlier in this book, for we must look for certain factors in the passage. Is spiritual disease pictured, and is sin reflected, or ignorance, or alienation from God? Is there anything to resemble spiritual deadness or injury, or the receiving of spiritual life? Or is there any allusion to atonement, or anything about judgement, or Heaven or hell, or God's mercy? In addition – and this is very important – do we see any special arguments to persuade lost souls, or is any particular kind of sinner in view?

If we keep in mind a mental list of these vital elements of the Gospel, we will not fail to identify them. 'But,' the protest comes, 'this is not interpretation, but the reading in of our presuppositions.' Of course it is, but when the Saviour tells us that this is what parables convey, it becomes a legitimate and necessary pursuit, and any other procedure is vain. We must bring presuppositions and expectations to the Word of God, as long as they are the expectations prescribed in the Word.

The parable of the good Samaritan is usually held up by modern approach teachers as an example of a *moral* story of Christ, with no possible evangelistic content. It is taken this way by all modern evangelical books on the parables. (Only *sometimes* do past preachers take it this way.) Some years ago the writer received a letter from a prominent evangelical pastor critical of a published 'evangelistic' exposition of this parable. He said it was a breach of all sane rules of interpretation to see Christ as the Samaritan. It was unwarranted allegorisation.

How, then, do we arrive at a gracious (or Gospel) message in this parable? To begin with, we are guided by the rule that all Christ's parables are gracious according to the texts already considered. Alongside this, we remember the 'fuse' attached to the parables. They all possess, to some extent, a delayed-action understandability. With Christ's crucifixion and resurrection, all take on a clearer meaning and stand ready to supply arguments and appeals to the preaching of the Gospel. The parable of the good Samaritan had a fuse attached, so that the scribe to whom it was spoken, and all within hearing, would grasp its meaning a little later.

As the parable was given in answer to a question, we need to consider the kind of answer the Lord might give to someone who asked, 'What shall I do to inherit eternal life?' Would He really have left the questioner with nothing better than – perform the commandments 'and thou shalt live'? It is, of course, inconceivable that the Saviour of souls would give no greater light.

As we begin to study the parable, perhaps for message preparation, another scripture containing the word 'Samaritan' comes to our attention, in *John 8.47-48*, where the Lord reproves the Jewish leaders and scribes, and they reply, 'Say we not well that thou art a Samaritan, and hast a devil?' Their words show that many of them were using this term of abuse to describe the Lord, doubtless in private and in public, and now they hurl it in His face as if to justify it. In due time, when Christ (Who was known for compassion and good works) went to Calvary, rose again, and began to be preached about by the apostles as the rescuer and Saviour of wounded, dying men and women, the hearers of this parable would say to themselves, '*He* was the good Samaritan. He spoke of Himself. We called Him a Samaritan, and we despised Him, but all the time He was tending the wounds of lost people like us.'

The Lord's provocative and inflammatory story, casting the Jewish clergy in so bad a light, would have been driven deeply into the memories of hearers and it would live again as Gospel events unfolded. As *Isaiah 53* became fulfilled before their eyes, they would say, 'He provided for us in our sin, spiritual loss, and hopelessness. He poured into the wounds of our sin and guilt the oil and wine of free forgiveness, set us on His own beast, and carried us to safety.'

We have read sermons from past pulpit worthies describing the man on the downhill journey from Jerusalem to Jericho as picturing a sinner on his progressive descent into sin. Such sermons have presented the notorious route, and the ambush as picturing attack by thieves such as immorality, atheism, materialistic thinking and self-love. We have read some perhaps less warranted applications of, say, the oil and the wine and the two coins, but the imaginative excesses of some should not lead to the abandoning of saving grace in the story.

This parable unmistakeably shows the unexpected, unappreciated saving mission of Christ; His immense compassion; His readiness to save; His treatment of our injuries; His sure comforts; His strengthening of the wounded; His continuing care; and His bearing of all the cost of our rescue. Who has the compassion to save, in this parable – the priesthood, or the despised One?

The preacher's task is to identify such gracious elements of the story together with any distinctive reasoning for lost sinners. In his presentation he will need to preserve the story-form because this is its fascinating strength. Some preachers seem anxious to turn every parable into a kind of physics lesson, giving a didactic series of points, and leaving no trace of a story once told.

It is said that Calvin refused to spiritualise parables, rejecting, for example, that the good Samaritan pictured Christ. It is true that the great expositor was inclined to overreact against the extreme Catholic allegorisation of the parables, and that he expounded them extremely briefly. (Calvin's exposition of the Gospels amounts to a single volume *harmony*.) One modern approach author provides an unwitting acknowledgement that the vast majority of Reformation tradition preachers *did* spiritualise the parables, when he calls Calvin a 'lone voice' in the matter until the latter part of the nineteenth century. Calvin, however, does point out the Gospel in parables, in his own way, as demonstrated in his treatment of the prodigal son, where he widens his application to include – God's boundless goodness and readiness to forgive; God's call to men to repent; God meeting the sinner as soon as he proposes to confess his guilt; the nature of repentance; and the illustration of how the 'best robe' buries the Father's view of sin.

As a means of communicating the Gospel a parable is remarkably helpful, because it strangely opens the mind of even a hostile hearer. Let us suppose the preacher seeks to engage the attention of unsaved people in a more direct way, crying, 'You are a sinner! You will go to hell! You need redemption! You must repent in shame!' In a sense something like this must be done, but if it is the first or exclusive element in evangelistic preaching, the preacher will quickly antagonise many hearers.

The genius of the parable is that it places the 'iron fist' of the Gospel in a velvet glove, for instead of crying: 'You! you! you!' it focuses attention on a person in a parable, who represents the needy, lost sinner. It softens the sharp edge of the Gospel in such a way that it will be heard by people – even cynical and hostile people – without immediate personal offence. The application may then be made progressively. So the preacher is very glad of parables (as he is of miracles) because they provide a fascinating framework for the Gospel that will engage the listener, enable the compassion of the Gospel to be sensed and make the potentially offensive thrust of a spiritual assault bearable and effective.

Another great value of the parable to the preacher is that it is clearly *the Lord's* teaching, and so the preacher does not come across as one presenting his own ideas. Nor does he need to include a battery of quotations to prove his message, as if he were presenting an academic paper, because his sermon is obviously only amplifying something given by the Lord. The preacher is but a representative of a higher authority, and however young he may be, he will not be resented as an upstart. How valuable are parables to Gospel messengers! How tragic it is that even Bible-believing seminaries are

turning out students trained to be cynical – sometimes even con-
temptuous – of the greatest source of soul-winning arguments
available to them, namely, the choice sermons of the Son of God.
The modern approach has a lot to answer for.

Miracles and the Gospel

It is equally a tragic loss to the ministry when the evangelistic
purpose of Christ's miracles is scrapped, for these mighty wonders
were 'parables in action' designed to portray the Lord dealing with
spiritually sick and dying people. The Lord certainly performed
miracles to prove He was divine, and also to manifest His boundless
compassion, but equally to demonstrate the miracle and method of
conversion.

Miracles are described in the *Gospel of John* as 'signs', signifying or
illustrating something. We realise they point to Christ's deity, but
clearly also to something more, because they are so elaborate and
precise, and are invested by the Lord with explanatory words such as
'faith', and 'saved'. To the woman who touched the hem of His garment the Lord said, 'Daughter, thy faith hath made thee whole; go in
peace'; to the two blind men, 'According to your faith be it unto
you'; to the Syrophoenician woman, 'O woman, great is thy faith: be
it unto thee even as thou wilt'; to the centurion whose servant was
dying, 'I have not found so great faith, no, not in Israel'; and to the
grateful Samaritan leper, 'Arise, go thy way: thy faith hath made thee
whole.'

Speaking to the blind man at Jericho, the Lord referred both to
faith and being saved, saying 'Receive thy sight: thy faith hath saved
thee.' He used the identical words, significantly, when speaking to a
woman who had received no miraculous healing, but who had been
forgiven. The woman who anointed His feet with ointment was
told, 'Thy faith hath saved thee; go in peace.'

The mixing of faith with the miracles shows that these are more than tokens of Godhead, but acts which signified, resembled, symbolised or paralleled the saving activity of Christ. They are specimens or pictures of conversion and its terms, and have been called by some, 'enacted parables' and 'sermons in action'.

The disciples on the Emmaus road called the Lord 'a prophet mighty in deed and word', realising that He taught through His miracles as well as His preaching. He told the future apostles that after His ascension they would do greater works than His miracles, by which He meant they would be used by the Spirit in the work of *spiritual* regeneration and healing, His own unsurpassed miracles being physical symbols of spiritual new birth.

Miracles, therefore, teach *how* Christ saves souls, and *on what terms*. We cannot help noticing that the Lord sometimes mixes a healing miracle with a salvation message, as in the case of the paralysed man let down through the roof of a house by four friends *(Luke 5.18-26)*. The Lord said, 'Man, thy sins are forgiven thee,' and the scribes and Pharisees became angry about His supposed blasphemy. The Saviour proceeded to ask them whether it was easier to say, 'Thy sins be forgiven thee', or 'Rise up and walk', relating the physical healing to spiritual healing. Then He pronounced the words: 'But that ye may know that the Son of man hath power upon earth to forgive sins . . . I say unto thee, Arise, and take up thy couch, and go into thine house.' This is the Lord providing a virtual interpretation of the miracle, showing that the physical healing pictured spiritual new life through forgiveness.

Another occasion when the Saviour showed that His miracles were 'specimens' of salvation was the healing of the man born blind in *John 9*. The disciples asked whose sin had given rise to the blindness, that of the parents or the man himself. The Lord, of course, corrected their thinking and made a momentous statement about the purpose of miracles. 'Jesus answered, Neither hath this man sinned, nor his parents: but that the works of God should be made manifest in him.' The reason for the man's blindness was that the works or miracles, in which love, mercy and restoration were shown, might be revealed or displayed in him. The plural 'works' refers not just to the restoration of sight, but all that this represents. The words 'made manifest' mean revealed, declared, or fully displayed, speaking of a visual representation of something.

Before the healing, Christ said, 'As long as I am in the world, I am the light of the world,' and this grand statement can mean nothing other than that the healing would be a demonstration of His method of bringing light to a dark world, by imparting spiritual sight to lost souls. The Lord made clay or mud, smeared it on the eyes of the blind man (surely as a symbol of the defilement of guilt) and bade him wash in the Pool of Siloam, 'which is by interpretation, Sent'. This was either a symbol of Himself, the 'sent' Saviour, or a memorial of the miraculous deliverance given to Jerusalem when the Angel of the Lord destroyed Sennacherib's army. Every citizen of Jerusalem would have associated the Pool of Siloam with the idea of deliverance.

The man humbled himself and washed in order to receive healing. Was this miracle really a lesson in receiving spiritual sight? Of course, because the Lord applied this very message to the watching Pharisees with the words, 'For judgment I am come into this world, that they which see not might see; and that they which see might be made blind.' These Pharisees knew only too well that He spoke of *spiritual* sight, because they replied, 'Are we blind also?'

Why did the Lord heal the man with an unclean spirit (a deeply immoral demonisation) if it were not to show moral reformation by conversion? Even the last frantic kick of the demon corresponds to the last flailings of fleshly resistance to an overwhelming work of grace in the heart. We could review so many miracles to prove the point and to establish the full sense of John's words –

'And many other signs truly did Jesus in the presence of his disciples, which are not written in this book: but these are written, that
ye might believe that Jesus is the Christ, the Son of God; and that
believing ye might have life through his name' *(John 20.30-31).*

Did the apostle only mean that the miracles would prove Christ's
divinity and thus encourage our belief? Or did he also mean that the
record of miracles would illustrate and 'declare' the way of salvation, 'that believing ye might have life through his name'? The latter,
without doubt, is the case, and this gracious purpose is present in all
the miracles.

Most teachers of the modern approach, while accepting the message of the Gospel themselves, do not see it in most of the miracles
of Christ, and thus take away from their students a deep store of
evangelistic persuasion and arguments vital to soul-winning. Like
our Lord's parables, the miracles have a fuse attached to them, their
full light bursting forth after the Saviour's death and resurrection.
As with parables, we recommend the reading of Spurgeon on the
miracles, as well as scores of other published sermons from the past,
to learn from the long tradition of using them as vehicles for the
Gospel. How perfectly an old Congregationalist hymnwriter put it –

Lord, I was blind, I could not see
In Thy marred visage any grace;
But now the beauty of Thy face
In radiant vision dawns on me.

Lord, I was deaf, I could not hear
The thrilling music of Thy voice;
But now I hear Thee and rejoice,
And sweet are all Thy words, and dear.

For Thou hast made the blind to see,
The deaf to hear, the dumb to speak,
The dead to live; and so, I break
The chains of my captivity.

William Tidd Matson (1833-99)

11

Positive Steps of Interpretation
With examples of classic wrong-turnings

'NO PROPHECY of the scripture is of any private interpretation,' Peter tells us, indicating that we have no right to
form instant, dogmatic, personal opinions when seeking
the meaning of a biblical passage. Here we review six rules or steps
for interpretation, with examples to show how their neglect has led
to notoriously wrong conclusions. In times when record numbers of
'isms' are sweeping into Bible-believing churches, are we using such
basic rules for interpreting texts?

This chapter is not a practical guide for message preparation, but a
more general review of Bible interpretation suitable for all readers
who would like a bird's-eye-view for the resolution of problems, as
well as for the serious study of the Word. (See Appendix I – Twenty-
One Steps for Message Preparation, page 145.)

The Bible is not so confusing that different teachers are bound to
interpret it in a variety of ways. Some evangelical writers claim that
God has built an element of confusion into His Word because He
wants His people to come to their own conclusions, no matter how

1 PRAYER & REVERENCE

2 AVOID WRONG ATTITUDES
  i   Self-justification
  ii Need to win argument
  iii Unduly technical spirit
  iv Superficial spirit

3 COMMITMENT TO ACCURACY
  i   Observe detail
  ii Exact meaning of words

4 THE SENSIBLE SENSE FIRST
  i   The plain sense
  ii   The appropriate sense
       for the type of book
  iii The context

5 THE TEST OF SOUND DOCTRINE
  i   Agreement with all doctrine
  ii   Compare with other passages
  iii Is it part of a larger whole?
  iv   In more than one place
  v   No proof outside the Bible

6 FOLLOW DIRECTIVE FACTORS

USE OF COMMENTARIES

many different viewpoints come about. Such claims muddy the waters, putting across the notion that this large, mysterious, complex book – the Bible – cannot be precisely interpreted, and contains no exact instructions for the organisation of the church or the conduct of individual and church life. But God has given us a supernatural and self-consistent book, sufficient for all the needs of His people, and so perfect that, provided we observe rules of honesty and diligence, we may come to right conclusions. Any failure will always be due to us, not to God's Word.

1 POSITIVE STEPS OF INTERPRETATION
Prayer and Reverence

The first rule for interpreting Scripture and for testing any teaching is the most obvious, yet it is frequently allowed to slip. Whenever we study God's Word we must begin with *prayer, genuine reverence and humility.* 'No prophecy of the scripture is of any private interpretation . . . but holy men of God spake as they were moved by the Holy Ghost,' says Peter, and we need the help of that same Spirit to understand God's Word. Peter also says, 'Gird up the loins of your mind, be sober.' Lay aside, he exhorts, all wrong attitudes and desire the milk of the Word with sincerity and with the humble openness and desire of a newborn baby.

We must pray for illumination, but this does not mean revelation. We should not ask for a revelation in which the meaning floats down to us from Heaven, dawning on our mind by divine communication. We must pray for the illuminating blessing of the Spirit to help and guide our diligent application of the biblical rules.

We know that the Bible provides an objective standard for all aspects of faith and life, not having a unique meaning for each individual Christian, but one meaning intended by God for everyone. We pray that we may see and grasp that message. Over-confidence is particularly disastrous for Bible study, growing too readily alongside our increasing familiarity with the Word. Humility alone breeds care, patience and openness to teaching.

We shall certainly grieve the Spirit and lose His help if we do not also come to the Bible with reverence. We must say to ourselves, 'This is God's Word; this is the Truth by which I will be judged; this is my Saviour's book of commands to me, and my attitude to it cannot be separated from my attitude to Him.' However long we may have been in the faith, we make many foolish mistakes if we leap into the Word without adequate prayer and reverence.

2 POSITIVE STEPS OF INTERPRETATION
Avoid Wrong Attitudes

The second rule for interpretation of the Bible is to free ourselves from *several wrong attitudes*, these being listed under four sub-points.

The first wrong attitude to be disposed of is *the aim or desire to justify an existing opinion*. Anything may be proved from the Word of God if we come only to confirm a pre-existing opinion. We must bring the biblical expectations noted in earlier chapters, but not firm opinions arrived at from our personal judgement, or picked up from other people and never subjected to biblical testing.

The second (and related) wrong attitude is a burning *need to win an argument*, where the mind is closed and the contender is driven by a competitive urge to get a victory over an adversary. Scripture is then frantically combed and consulted in order to carry the debate and 'keep face'.

The third wrong attitude is that of *an unduly technical spirit*. The great interest of some Christians seems to be in dates and places, in history and geography, or in technically controversial passages. Some commentators engage so minutely in technical aspects that they miss the wood for the trees and see no spiritual message in the text. The interpreter certainly has work to do to establish the correct meaning of words in their context, but we should avoid an unduly technical approach.

The fourth wrong attitude to avoid is *a superficial spirit*, which snatches at the most obvious sense only. The first thing that occurs to us is not necessarily the whole picture, and if we rest content with that, never considering the details and the implications, we will probably miss the real point. The most remarkable mistake of modern approach teachers, as we noted earlier, is that having exhausted themselves with technical procedures, they settle for tame superficiality when considering the meaning and application of passages. We need to look for all the doctrines and duties in the passage, taking special note of possible rebukes or encouragements.

3 POSITIVE STEPS OF INTERPRETATION
Commitment to Accuracy

Our third rule of interpretation is that we must be *committed to accuracy*. Here we offer two sub-points.

We must *observe detail*. Some years ago a well-known charismatic preacher produced a best-selling book in which he claimed that 'power encounters' were essential to evangelism. He was keen that everyone should be able to work miracles and have words of knowledge in order to impress unbelievers and open their minds to the Gospel. In justification of this idea, he asserted that there was not a single evangelistic encounter in the New Testament which did not have a miracle of some kind attached to it. Every one, he claimed, was accompanied by some act of power; some supernatural wonder. However, if the author had looked more carefully, he would have found that the New Testament records many acts of witness unaccompanied by miracles. He noticed that wonders and witness were connected together in some cases, and assumed that this was true of every case, and soon an entire philosophy of witness was built without the detail being checked. This is just one example of many quite major departures from orthodox Christianity which have arisen from neglect of detail.

A similar case in point is the frequency of miracles in the time of the New Testament. Charismatic believers are usually taught that the New Testament church was awash with signs, wonders and healings, and that virtually every Christian everywhere could perform them. Surely, they reason, such wonders should be equally manifested today. The conclusion sounds obvious and compelling, but as soon as one looks more closely at the New Testament data, a discovery is made, namely, that with one exception, no healing was ever performed other than by the hands of an apostle or an apostolic deputy. (Philip and Stephen worked miracles and some say Barnabas did also, but the text used in support of the latter is inconclusive.)

Paul says that the apostles were given healing power in order to authenticate them as apostles. If all believers could heal, how would the apostles have been authenticated? We read of Peter going about performing wonders, raising one person and restoring another, and in each case an entire region is stunned and amazed. An apostle performs a healing miracle and people flock from far and wide. A young lad falls out of a window at Troas and the congregation is stricken with horror because neither elders nor members can do anything about it. Only an apostle can heal the boy.

Charismatic believers, however, are mostly under the impression that miracles were commonly performed by many people, and this idea has become the lens through which they look at the New Testament. More detailed study provides a quite different picture from that which is so often painted.

Many popular Christian books today employ a highly superficial technique of interpretation, introducing each chapter with a text, then making no further reference to it. The impression is conveyed that the book is thoroughly biblical, but in reality no detailed attention is given even to the texts quoted. Without any sensible reasoning the text is claimed to mean such and such, and the author then proceeds to exhort readers in the light of his own opinions. Spiritual shepherds should watch out for such books and warn believers about them, for attention to detail must be the hallmark of sound teaching.

The second sub-point of commitment to accuracy is that the student of the Bible should take care to determine the *exact meaning of words*, particularly of crucial, pivotal words. Another example of a mistake from the charismatic scene concerns the anointing of the sick with oil in *James 5*, often assumed to be a vital symbol representing the imparting or work of the Spirit in the act of healing.

Even without a knowledge of New Testament Greek it is possible to consult a dictionary or commentary and see that James did not choose the 'religious' word for anointing, but a very secular word, meaning simply to apply oil (as they did medicinally to treat sores). James literally says – 'oiling with oil'. In other words, he tells elders not to be too spiritually minded to be of any earthly use, urging them to attend to the sufferer's bodily needs. They may even have taken a nurse with them to apply the oil. By extension, elders in a cold climate should ensure that a sick person has food and warmth.

The oil also shows that medication is appropriate alongside prayer.

Many preachers build nearly all their sermons on careful word explanations, and this can be immensely profitable (as long as there is full application), but whatever the sermon style, correct word meanings are crucial.

4 POSITIVE STEPS OF INTERPRETATION
The Sensible Sense First

The fourth rule of interpretation is expressed here in non-technical language. We must first seek out the *sensible sense* of a passage, and this will be explained under three sub-points.

The first 'sensible sense' sub-point is that we should observe very carefully *the plain sense* of the text, taking in the most obvious meaning of the passage. The spiritual meaning and application must never become detached from the plain sense.

The writer has already argued that the old term 'grammatical-historical approach' has been redefined with new meaning by modern approach advocates, so that it effectively destroys the divine character of the Bible. As we have seen, they have limited the expositor's work by saying that his sole aim is to establish what the original human author meant to say to his contemporary hearers. The Bible ceases to convey a profound divine message channelled through authors who often did not fully comprehend what they were writing.

To understand the plain sense of the passage is essential, though it is not the *only* step, for the inspired authors often spoke more profoundly than they realised. God both orchestrated their history and gave them words paralleling and reflecting the gracious work of Christ and the spiritual walk of Gospel age believers. There are, for example, many wonderful events throughout the Old Testament where the plain sense will only relate *what* happened, but we must then discern with the help of New Testament light *why* it happened, and what doctrines were being demonstrated, and what pastoral lessons taught. We will also seek *types* of Christ, or prophecies. In short, two potential mistakes may be mentioned here, one being the tendency to ride roughshod over the plain sense, reading fanciful meanings into the text, and the other looking no further than the plain sense, as though the Bible were a history book only.

The second sub-point under 'sensible sense' is that we must ask what is the *appropriate sense for the kind of book.* For example, we read *Genesis* very differently from *Revelation,* because the former is history, while the latter is full of symbolic language, as the text makes clear. When we read about a bottomless pit, or about an angel with a great chain in his hand, we do not say that this is literally how it is, for these are symbols of the realities.

Many commentaries and Bible dictionaries packaged as 'evangelical' reveal their liberal views at this fundamental level. They tell you that *Genesis* is a history book, then promptly deny it, saying that the six-day creation is not literal but is nothing more than an analogy, because people in earliest times would not have understood a scientific account of creation. In explaining Noah's Flood we find much the same evasion of literal history, the deluge being reduced to a little local flood, and the powerful adjectives of the Bible dismissed as colourful. *Genesis,* however, presents itself as an historical book, not an allegory, and although it contains many types and parallels, they are implicit in the historical events that literally happened.

Ecclesiastes is by Solomon, the inspired master of parables, figures and allegory, and we look for the significance of each one. The same must be said of *Proverbs* and also *Song of Solomon,* viewed throughout most of the history of the church by believing expositors as an allegory showing the mutual love of Christ and His church. In the prophetic books we see the coming of Christ predicted and the character and blessedness of the church of the Gospel age, and also the Lord's return and the eternal glory. *Appropriate sense* means that we always respect the type of book that the Holy Spirit has written, or we come to wholly mistaken conclusions.

The third sub-point of seeking the 'sensible sense', probably the most ignored rule of all, is that we must examine every passage *in its context*. We could refer to so many examples of this being ignored, but we shall be limited to three. In *Matthew 7* the Lord says:

> 'Judge not, that ye be not judged. For with what judgment ye judge, ye shall be judged: and with what measure ye mete, it shall be measured to you again.'

Over thirty years ago, the author having preached a sermon which included criticism of an error, he was approached by a young theological student with a complaint. Lifting up his Bible in a dramatic manner, he said in stentorian tones: 'I have a message from the Lord for you . . .' and read out this very verse. Apparently, it was quite wrong for a preacher to warn against any error, because the Lord said, 'Judge not.'

This is a very commonly held view of the Saviour's words. However, if that brother had only looked at his chosen text in its context, he would have realised that he had drawn the wrong sense from it. He saw it as a command never to be critical; never to use discernment; never to consider whether any religious viewpoint is right or wrong. If only he had read the passage a little further he would have come across verse 6 – 'Give not that which is holy unto the dogs.' But if it is always wrong to assess anything, how are we to know who these unworthy people are?

The real meaning of the Lord is identified in verse 5 – 'Thou hypocrite, first cast out the beam out of thine own eye; and then shalt thou see clearly to cast out the mote out of thy brother's eye.' It is not the use of Christian discernment, nor disapproval of wrong conduct or views that is condemned, but the judging of others when we are guilty of the same (or greater) error. The stern seminarian should have read the nearby fifteenth verse: 'Beware of false prophets.' We need much discernment to detect false prophets because they 'come to you in sheep's clothing'. The chapter is full of the duty of discernment, and provides a classic example of the need to consider the context carefully.

Another example of failure to consider context is seen in pietistic teaching about how to grow in holiness. This has been around a long time, but a huge growth in support began toward the end of the nineteenth century, and since then countless books have advocated such teaching. Sanctification, it boldly asserts, is by faith, in the sense that the Holy Spirit will make us holy by Himself, if we will only stop fighting the battle ourselves and leave it to Him. Supportive texts are selected from places such as *Romans 6.1-11* and *Romans 7.1-11*, and particularly *Galatians 2.20* – all such texts apparently endorsing the view that sanctification is obtained in the same way as justification – by faith, as a gracious work of God.

However, if the context of the selected proof texts is seriously inspected, it is seen at once that they are not talking about sanctification, but justification. If one selects proof texts on sanctification from passages dealing with justification, one is bound to imagine that both are obtained in the same way. The interpretation of the texts sincerely offered by teachers of sanctification-by-faith collapses as soon as their context is considered, and the theme of the surrounding verses recognised.

Another example of the mistakes that occur when the context is neglected is that of healing. From *James 5* many people teach that Christian people have a right to be healed by the Lord, and certainly will be if they pray with sufficient faith. But once again, the context (stretching back into the preceding chapter) provides a correct understanding, for *James 4.15* places a banner headline across all that follows: 'For that ye ought to say, *If the Lord will,* we shall live, and do this, or that.' Does James abandon this bedrock principle – 'If the Lord will' – within a few verses to say that we have an *absolute right* to healing? Teachers who speak about a right to healing should have read the verses preceding their 'proof text'. Context is vital.

5 POSITIVE STEPS OF INTERPRETATION
The Test of Sound Doctrine

Our fifth rule of interpretation (drawn from the analogy of faith as we defined it earlier) means that every correct understanding or interpretation of a text will agree with the whole faith, or the teaching of the whole Bible. Considering the immense importance of this rule, it is amazing that it is not widely taught today. It rests on the fact that there can be no contradiction in the Bible. This rule is so vital that we must explain it under five sub-headings, with examples of mistakes.

The sub-points will be –

(i)   an interpretation must be checked against the whole doctrinal scheme of the Bible;

(ii) then checked with other scriptures on the same subject;

(iii) then checked to determine if the passage conveys an entire doctrine or duty or only a part of it – the remainder being spread across other texts;

(iv) then checked as to whether it is taught in more than one place;

(v) finally, our interpretation must not depend on non-biblical information.

Firstly, every interpretation must *agree with the entire system of doctrine* in the Bible. Many doctrines are taught repeatedly in the Word of God and are clearly beyond controversy. These may be drawn together and set out in systematic order, so that we can say, '*This* is the faith.' Great confessions of faith, particularly those such as the Westminster Confession, Baptist Confession (Second London) and Savoy Confession of the seventeenth century stand as admirable statements of such key doctrines of the Word.

In the study of any passage, if we arrive at an understanding which contradicts these settled and indisputable doctrines taught in many places in the Bible, we will know we are mistaken. If, for example, we find a passage which seems to say that Christians can lose their salvation, and we compare this possibility with our established, sound statement of doctrine (teaching the contrary), grounded on numerous texts, we will be warned that we have misunderstood the passage, because the Bible cannot contradict itself.

When the present writer was a fairly new believer, he heard a discussion between other young people on the subject of election. Some held that many Bible verses taught free will, while others held that many texts taught unconditional election. After animated argument it was agreed that if someone would count up the number of texts on each side of the argument, the side with the most texts would be declared victorious and correct. In a way, the proposed solution was in the right direction, but it still missed the point, because it implied that the minority texts must be wrong, whereas the Bible is never wrong.

There is no doubt that election is very plainly stated many times throughout the Bible, and has the 'majority' of texts. If, therefore, we find a text that *appears* to teach free will, we must understand it in the light of election. For example, some free will texts describe God's offer of salvation from man's point of view, saying, if we turn to Him for mercy, He will receive us. Other texts, however, explain what lies behind a sincere and repentant response to God, showing that it is the Lord Who opens the sinner's heart and inclines his will. As far as the sinner's subjective experience is concerned, he chooses, and apparently freely. But behind his choosing is the work of the Spirit, based on election. Election is the explanation, free will is the human effect. The sinner chooses only because God has mercifully worked in his heart. The two families of text are perfectly consistent, as long as the free will texts are seen to be the subjective human aspect of God's sovereign, electing, overruling work.

Another example of the need to check one's understanding of a text against the whole body of doctrine, is the case of whether *Hebrews 6.4-6* contradicts the doctrine of eternal security. The passage seems to suggest that a believer can fall away from God, saying:

> 'For it is impossible for those who were once enlightened, and have tasted of the heavenly gift, and were made partakers of the Holy Ghost, and have tasted the good word of God, and the powers of the world to come, if they shall fall away, to renew them again unto repentance . . .'

The first time this writer read *Hebrews 6*, many years ago as a new believer, it seemed to say that believers could be lost. Later, however, it became obvious that this understanding brought the text into collision with the doctrine of eternal security – a basic teaching of the faith. A more careful examination of the passage, no doubt helped by a commentary, revealed the illustration of two fields, one of which would soon produce a good crop, and the other thorns and briars. At one stage, in the early spring perhaps, both appeared to be bare, brown fields. One had been sown, and the other not, but before shoots appeared, both fields were alike. As time went by, however, when wheat grew in one, and thorns in the other, the real character of each field was revealed, and its 'true nature' known. The illustration of the fields shows that the difference between professing Christians who stand and those who fall is the presence or absence of saving 'seed' in the heart. If precious seed has been sown there, eternal fruit will be borne. Once the text is considered in the light of the doctrine of final perseverance, we then learn new facts from it, in this case the extent to which unconverted people may receive a measure of light and conviction without truly repenting and finding Christ.

The first sub-heading for the analogy of faith is that our inter-pretation of any passage must agree with the body of doctrines established from throughout the Bible.

The second sub-point to the analogy of faith is that any study of a passage must include its *comparison with other scriptures on the same subject.* The following is an example of people omitting to compare scriptures. We often hear it said that the apostle Paul failed in his work when he was in Athens, so that his ministry faltered. Then he went to Corinth and re-evaluated his methods, changing them dramatically. There he began (so it is said) to use wonders and miracles as the cornerstone of his evangelism, and failure instantly turned into success. This idea is based on the record of his supposed new policy given in *1 Corinthians 2.4 –*

> 'And my speech and my preaching was not with enticing words of man's wisdom, but in demonstration of the Spirit and of power.'

However, if teachers of this scenario would only compare Scrip-ture with Scripture, in this case comparing *1 Corinthians 2.4* with *Acts 17-18* where Paul's work in Athens and Corinth is narrated they would realise their interpretation was wrong. Luke's highly detailed narrative in *Acts* reveals no change whatsoever in Paul's method from one place to the other.

In fact, Luke does not mention anything about signs and wonders either at Athens or Corinth, but he does say that Paul 'reasoned' with and 'persuaded' people at Corinth, just as he had at Athens. Paul's supposed failure and change of approach would never have been dreamed up if the parallel passage had been consulted.

Further, if these teachers honoured the rule of context, they would notice that just in front of their *1 Corinthians 2* text, there is half a chapter of powerful reasoning showing that the power of God to save operates exclusively through the preaching of the cross, and not through signs or wonders (see *1 Corinthians 1.17-31*). How is it possible to miss such a famous and inspiring context? If Paul did change his policy, as they claim, he certainly did not seem to know he had done so. This example completes our second point – that any interpretation or teaching must be consistent with other scriptures speaking of the same subject.

The third sub-point of the analogy of faith is this: If the passage being studied presents a doctrine or duty, we must ask, *does it convey an entire doctrine or duty, or only part of it*? This is a little different from simply checking one text against another. This sub-point says that we must bring *all* the passages which speak about any doctrine together because each may contribute some different facet or aspect of it. If we take only one or some of these passages without the others, we may obtain a distorted picture.

An obvious example of failing to consult other texts is seen in the sad story of the so-called 'Jesus freaks' in California (and to a far smaller extent in England) during the early 1970s. Hippies professing conversion formed themselves into communes and had 'all things common', guided, they believed, by the community of goods in the *Acts of the Apostles*, the book which was their sole source of information for their conduct as Christians. They did not know, and no one seemed to show them, that the doctrine of the church is to be built up from a number of passages, and especially from the epistles. All must be studied together, and each contributes to the full picture. This rule is of particular importance in arriving at the biblical mode of church government.

The fourth sub-point for the analogy of faith is that any important doctrine or practice will be *taught in more than one place*. There are many examples of mistakes made at this point, such as sincere and sound churches who believe in washing feet at the Lord's Table. This is certainly not something that could be regarded as a serious and harmful misinterpretation, but it serves to illustrate the point, for the practice is entirely based on one text and this should have led to caution. Because footwashing at the Lord's Supper appears in only one passage (the washing of the disciples' feet by the Lord) it most probably describes a singular act of the Lord symbolising the humility and service that disciples should show towards each other. We should be careful not to build a practice on one text.

The same goes for the idea of speaking in tongues for private benefit, or speaking in ecstatic tongues at all (that is tongues which resemble no known language). Such ideas are derived from only one passage of Scripture – two verses within *1 Corinthians 14*. Private and ecstatic tongues are not seen in *Acts* (only public tongues of real languages), nor in any epistle outside *1 Corinthians*, nor are there any instructions about this in the pastoral epistles, and this should lead the serious Bible student to examine the text with special care. This extra diligence leads us to notice that other verses in *1 Corinthians 14* contradict the idea. Paul says that if we do not speak words that edify others, the gift is useless, and if people cannot understand us, we are no better than barbarians, both statements negating private and ecstatic tongues speaking. Millions of Christians are today practising things only hinted at in a single passage of Scripture, and sometimes movements have been built on such slender foundations.

The fifth sub-point for the analogy of faith is simple, but very necessary today. We must ask whether we have arrived at a certain interpretation or teaching because we have used or been influenced by *information from outside the Bible.* If we had confined our study to the Bible, would we come to our conclusion? This does not mean that we never study the history, geography and culture of Bible times, all of which are richly informative and helpful, but it does mean that no interpretation should *depend* on extra-biblical information. Many evangelical commentators today form conclusions on the basis of what liberal academics think. Experts in ancient anthropology provide information which is trusted more than the Bible itself and is allowed to change the sense of the passage.

Cynical scholars assert that Moses copied and adapted God's laws and ceremonies from the culture of surrounding nations, and information drawn from those pagan laws is used to 'interpret' the Pentateuch. The Bible is the product of divine genius, given for every age, and has not waited for present-day unbelieving scholars to yield up its meaning.

If we cannot prove an idea from the Bible alone, we should drop it. When it comes to determining whether a doctrine or practice is right, we are to focus exclusively on the data provided within the Bible.

6 POSITIVE STEPS OF INTERPRETATION
Follow Directive Factors

Our sixth rule of interpretation is – *follow special instructions given in the Bible about certain texts or topics.* Are there any special guiding principles given in the Bible to influence or throw light on the passage being studied? This is another aspect of interpreting Scripture by Scripture, but it is so distinctive that it merits a special heading and explanation.

Biblical directions on handling various parts of the Bible include *1 Corinthians 10.1-12,* already examined, which instructs us to look for Christ and His church in the Old Testament. We therefore use the 'grid' of expectations described in chapter 5, the mind being primed to discern the types, the examples of godliness, obedience, and also faithlessness and disobedience. We look for types or parallels of Christ and His glorious person and work; for the presence of a doctrine, or for a pastoral message of correction or encouragement. *1 Corinthians 10.1-12* informs us about the purpose and content of the Pentateuch, indeed, about all the historical books of the Old Testament, training and directing students of the Word how to approach them.

Another example of a special instruction, already mentioned in this book, is *Hebrews 11*, which provides guiding information about how to view the spiritual status of patriarchs and other heroes of faith, including the judges, and indicating the extent of their light, and their aims.

A third example of a special instruction is the group of texts in which Paul tells us that everything that he does in the New Testament record is to be closely imitated, for he is God's instrument to bring into being the pattern church of the Gospel age. Though he was a man subject to sin, by God's overriding grace he never put a foot wrong in his organisation of the churches and his teaching ministry as revealed in Scripture. When the Spirit of Christ inspired the New Testament, He recorded only those things about Paul which provided a perfect example. Among the texts commanding imitation (literally *mimicking*) of Paul are these:

> 'Wherefore I beseech you, be ye followers of me'
> *(1 Corinthians 4.16).*

> 'Be ye followers of me, even as I also am of Christ'
> *(1 Corinthians 11.1).*

> 'Brethren, be followers together of me, and mark them which walk so as ye have us for an ensample' *(Philippians 3.17).*

In the light of these texts, when Barnabas disagreed with Paul over John Mark, Barnabas was in the wrong, and Paul was in the right. If we come to the opposite conclusion, it is because we have lost sight of the texts that direct how Paul's revealed actions should be viewed. Other arguments may be advanced to support Paul's case, but the directing passages are decisive.

When Agabus and other prophets urged Paul not to go to Jerusalem, they were wrong and he was right to go (which is obvious, because if prophecy said he would suffer, it equally predicted that he would be there). When Paul appointed Timothy and Titus as prototype pastors, he was acting by the direction of God in inaugurating a pattern of ministry for Gospel churches. We do not discuss dispassionately whether he was doing the wisest thing, because the 'imitate' texts inform us that he was providing an inspired example for all time. We may and must imitate everything that Paul did. If he arranged for the elders of churches to be elected by congregations, we must do the same, for he was the Lord's master-builder of a pattern church.

Yet another example of a special instruction is *John 20.30-31*, which calls miracles *signs*, and assigns to them an evangelistic purpose. In other words, there is grace in every miracle, and we should look for the distinctive evangelistic reasoning in each one, as we argue in chapter 10. The Saviour spoke also of His miracles indicating that they were pictures of His manner of saving souls from spiritual blindness, deafness, and disease, and these statements direct us to see the saving message in them and present it. These directing passages are also presented in chapter 10.

✳ ✳ ✳ ✳ ✳

Before closing this chapter on steps of interpretation, an additional rule may be added, which is to ask – 'What do the great commentators say?' Of course, they are not inspired, and not necessarily right, but if none of them agrees with us we should be warned, because the Bible is not so mysterious and difficult that in a period of 2,000 years no one else will have seen the meaning we assign to a passage. This simple rule is based on the perspicuity (easy understandability) of God's Word. It has been rightly said, 'If you think of something which no one has ever thought of before, don't think it.' We may be greatly helped and guided by many commentaries, but we will also be cautioned by them when an idea runs ahead of what has been grasped previously.

Armed with Bible-inspired rules of interpretation like these, the expositor will pray for God's grace to be a 'workman that needeth not to be ashamed, rightly dividing the word of truth'.

12

Is the Bible Always Binding for Today?
How to distinguish temporary from permanent duties

ONE OF THE most important needs in Bible interpretation is to know which commands or examples of behaviour are binding on Christian people today, and which are not. The question is often put in this form: How may we tell what is normative for today (that is: what texts are intended to establish a pattern or standard)? This question has never been more relevant, as we live at a time when numerous biblical standards are being discarded by many church leaders who appear to be evangelicals. Ordinary believers are utterly confused by the current scene, gaining the impression that the Bible is an unclear book which need not be taken seriously as far as its practical details are concerned. General obedience is enough.

It is certainly not correct to defend the authority of the Bible simply by saying – 'Everything in the Bible is to be obeyed,' because anyone can see that this is not so. The Old Testament ceremonial regulations, for example, are no longer in force. They are not normative for today. And what about the apparent command of Christ to wash one another's feet, or the exhortation of Paul to greet one another with a holy kiss? Are these to be literally obeyed in our time? And should we work only with our hands, as craftsmen and labourers, as the great apostle seems to say? And should Christians be able to do signs and wonders today, as the apostles did? Or should we sell our goods and distribute the proceeds, sharing all with fellow believers as they did in *Acts 2*?

Should we, like Paul, take a Nazarite vow? Should the Lord's Supper always be linked with a church fellowship meal, and held in the evening as it was with the first Christians? These questions bring us to the heart of the problem. If some of the practices of and apparent commands to the early church are not for today, and some are, how can we tell which is which? Where are we to draw the line between *binding* matters, and *non-binding* matters? Who is to say what is normative?

One of the reasons why *some* things are not literally binding on us today is that they were the *cultural* expressions of things commanded by God. The holy kiss, for example, was the accepted way of expressing peace and love in that culture, at that time. (We are told by some experts, incidentally, that it was only performed between people of the same sex.) In the West today the cultural equivalent is the warm handshake, and we generally say that the command of the apostle to greet one another with a holy kiss is to be obeyed *in principle*, using our culturally equivalent act.

However, this way of interpreting a command could give rise to serious mistakes. What about Paul's instruction that women should not preach or rule in the church? Some people claim that this was only commanded because the culture of the times required women to take a retiring role. If we can dispose of *literal* obedience to the holy kiss on the ground that it was a cultural expression of a duty, could we not dispose of the embargo on women in the ministry in the same way? This is exactly what is being said today about many other biblical commands or examples, and the Bible has lost much of its authority as a result.

If we look at some of the statements of faith drawn up by evangelicals in recent years we find sure evidence that there has been a considerable loss of respect for the authority of the Bible. Whereas the old statements of faith would speak about the Bible's *sufficiency* (meaning that it addressed *every* aspect of the life of the church), and also of its *authority* for all spiritual teaching and conduct, modern statements give the Bible a relatively small role. 'We believe,' they say, 'that the Scriptures are authoritative for salvation,' and then a full-stop draws to a close the role of the Bible. The Bible is no longer considered authoritative for all the conduct of the believer, or for the detailed organising of the church, but only for the message of salvation, and the Lord is no longer viewed as having any clear set of directions for His people.

If we ask some modern evangelical leaders why the Bible is no longer to be followed in its practical details they openly say that so much of it was subject to the culture of those times, and was, therefore, temporary. This has become the leading excuse made by many to justify indifference to the commands of the Bible.

To avoid this shallowness we need to have very clear standards by which we decide whether a biblical practice really was influenced by culture, and is, therefore, variable in its expression, or whether it was intended to be permanently binding and normative in the life of Christians and the church.

Sometimes the accusation that we are guilty of relegating parts of the Bible to the level of 'temporary truth' is levelled against those who reject the sign ministry of the charismatic movement. When we say that the sign-gifts of tongues-speaking and healing, not to mention the revelatory gifts of prophesying, were only for the foundation stage of the church, charismatic teachers say, 'You are limiting the Bible and saying that many things in the Bible are merely temporary, and not for today. You pick only what you want, and you reject the rest as being no longer binding.' Is this charge correct? Are signs and prophesyings for today?

How, then, may we determine whether commands or examples of conduct given in the Bible were temporary or permanent? Before we present the rule of interpretation we must employ, a word of clarification may be appreciated on two technical terms used on this subject. Theological writers often refer to the *regulative principle*. Broadly speaking this term expresses the belief that everything we do in Christian worship must be in exact accordance with the Word of God. If there is no precise command or clear example to do a particular thing, we must not do it, because we have no express warrant or authority.

This viewpoint is certainly better than the idea expressed in the *Thirty Nine Articles* of the Church of England, where it is said that the church has power to formulate any rites and ceremonies as long as they are not incompatible with, or contradictory to, the ethos of scriptural teaching. This is a very 'loose' standard which allows the church to stray down different liturgical bypaths and concoct all kinds of services of which there is no sign in the Scripture. The only control is that they must not be obviously *against* the Bible. The *regulative principle* is much stronger than this, insisting that there must be a specific authorisation in the Word for every part of our Christian worship.

However, the *regulative principle* does not go far enough, because this term only relates to *worship*, and we need a principle that governs not only worship, but *everything* the churches do, including how they govern themselves, how they evangelise and work, and so on. We need a principle that tells us how to distinguish between the temporary duties in the Bible, and the ongoing, binding ones. We will call this principle the *normative test*. Is something in the New Testament a command or pattern for the church to follow in detail, or is it a culture-bound practice, or temporary? The *normative test* is the method of interpretation that enables us to decide, and it is disarmingly simple.

At this point we must be aware that some evangelical teachers have suggested some surprising tests to determine what is binding. It has been claimed, for example, that Old Testament teaching and practice is only valid if it is repeated in the New. (Some claim that by this test the fourth commandment is no longer in force.) This test is obviously inadequate, because Christ treated all the Old Testament as the authoritative Word of God. Certainly the New Testament teaches that the ceremonial law was fulfilled and cancelled with the coming of Christ, but this is quite different from saying that *all* the Old Testament is cancelled *unless* it is repeated in the New.*

Here are tests which are consistent with the Bible, all of them clear and obvious, for deciding whether a thing either commanded or recorded as an example of conduct was intended to be temporary or permanent in the life of believers and the church.

1 **All Scripture is binding today unless Scripture itself cancels, limits or modifies what it prescribes.** Many passages, such as Old Testament historical narratives, record acts of God's people carried out in obedience to His commands – such as 'the church' going to war – which are not *literally* binding for today, because the record makes clear that they were God's will for that time and locality. This is usually too obvious to warrant discussion. All God's

---

*There are other very surprising tests suggested, even by some evangelicals, including the following. Texts in the Bible are only binding on Christians today if they are – (a) essential for salvation, (b) included in the life and teaching of Christ, (c) based on the nature of God, or (d) connected with the order of creation. We have no need to study these ideas except to say that they sweep away many of the detailed practical directions given to us in the epistles, which are claimed to be merely temporary. But these weak tests are usually advanced by so-called evangelicals who downgrade the Bible in other ways also.

ancient commands continue for today in a *spiritual* sense, referring, for example, to our fight against the world, the flesh and the devil. We have already noted that the New Testament cancels literal compliance with the ceremonial law of Moses.

Another example of something evidently limited is the task given to the apostles to carry out signs and wonders, because Luke says (twice in *Acts*) that these were exclusively performed by the hands of the apostles. We note, by contrast, that there is no limit of time and place put on the texts saying how churches should be governed. We are presented in the epistles with a 'pattern church', and there are no indications that this will ever need to be revised.

Another example of something being modified is Paul's especially strong exhortation to remain single in *1 Corinthians 7*. He goes on to say that 'this is good for the present distress' (verse 26). An example of a command which was modified some time after it was given is the list of duties given by the Lord to His disciples when He sent them out to the Jewish townships to proclaim His coming *(Matthew 10)*. They were to heal the sick, cleanse the lepers, raise the dead, and cast out devils, taking no money or change of clothing, but living by the hospitality of others. Are these 'marching orders' binding for preachers today? No, because they were radically revised by the Lord Himself at the close of His earthly ministry *(Luke 22.35-36)*.

2 **All Scripture is binding today unless the passage records immoral or irreligious behaviour.** This rule is obviously right, because the Bible would never command anything contrary to the Ten Commandments and other moral exhortations.

3 **All Scripture is binding today unless that which is required appears obscurely in one text only, and is not even hinted at elsewhere.** Once again we refer to the principle that Scripture must interpret itself, and that we must compare passages. If an apparent teaching is isolated and exclusive, it strongly suggests that we are wrong to identify it as a binding duty, because it cannot be verified by referring to other texts. This does not mean that the Bible texts are wrong, but that the practice recorded or instruction given was temporary or local. Some people say the Lord's Supper must be held every week, but others point out that this only appears in an observation about the practice at Troas, and receives no mention elsewhere. It could have been a local practice, and unlikely to be normative. It is important to ask the question, 'Is the duty or practice in more than one place?'

Literal obedience, or according to culture?

4 All Scripture is binding today unless it can be proved that the thing prescribed may be fully obeyed in different ways in different ages and cultures. May the *principle* be honoured by a different mode of expression? It is this point that will be explained in the remainder of the chapter.

We are using the word 'culture' to describe a distinctive way of life in a particular nation, region, or period. It refers (in these pages) to a package of social customs peculiar to a region. Unlike Islam, Christianity is not bound to one culture, but stands above culture. Spiritual and moral values are all-important, not rigid conformity to a distinctive outward set of manners or dress. When the Bible prescribes a practice for believers or churches, we must respect the spiritual and moral purpose behind what is prescribed, and ask whether the outward expression of that practice as performed in Bible times was cultural, and whether it could be expressed in a different way in another time and culture.

For example, to wash the feet of a guest (in the Bible) expressed humility coupled with courtesy, goodwill and helpfulness. In the culture of that age and region, these things were very well expressed in the kindness of footwashing, but it is the humility, courtesy, goodwill and helpfulness which are important, and these may be expressed in various ways. The washing of feet was the social custom of that time and place. In cold countries, where open footwear is not worn, and where the paths may not be dusty, footwashing is not part of the culture, and would be a very strange thing to do. It certainly would not be appreciated.

We ask ourselves therefore: is it necessary to adopt *this particular* expression of humility, courtesy, and kindness? Is footwashing essential to the obeying of God's will in this matter? Is it the only valid way of expressing the virtues listed? Most people would unhesitatingly say that it was not, because there is no unique spiritual significance to footwashing. It was only a practical courtesy of that region at that time. An important attitude and act of humility and courtesy was 'clothed' in a cultural coat, which could be changed.

The liberty to express a duty by a different outward act is in harmony with the spirit of texts such as *Philippians 3.3* – 'For we are the circumcision, which worship God in the spirit, and rejoice in Christ Jesus, and have no confidence in the flesh.' Christianity is not a religion of conformity to meticulous outward acts, except in the case of baptism and the Lord's Supper, which are symbolic acts uniquely ordained by Christ. *Romans 14.17* points in the same direction: 'For the kingdom of God is not meat and drink; but righteousness, peace, and joy in the Holy Ghost.' However, this line of reasoning does not sweep away detailed literal obedience to practical commands about, say, methods of church government, because these are part of God's design for His church, and are not symbolic.

To find out whether the *literal expression* of something as carried out in Bible times is binding for today, or whether the duty may be translated into today's culture, we must ask the following simple questions:

Question A. Was the act a social custom in Bible times?

Question B. Can the underlying principle or purpose be *equally* well expressed in some other way? (In other words, is the act carried out in Bible times the only way to express the principle?)

If the answer to both questions is 'yes', then the physical, outward act is cultural, and it is not necessary to carry out that act today, although the principle must be obeyed and expressed in the appropriate way for our time and culture.

If one or both of the questions is answered negatively, then the physical act of Bible times is still essential today. It has ongoing significance, and we should observe it. The chart entitled 'Tests for Whether a New Testament Instruction or Example is to be Literally Obeyed' (on page 108) shows eight examples of New Testament activities. The questions 'A' and 'B' are asked and answered. This is an elementary tool intended to demonstrate that there is a simple, 'scientific' way of deciding if the outward act of any biblical requirement was cultural, and subject to change.

Take the case of women who were not permitted to preach the Word to men, or to lead in the church. **Question A:** Was it a social custom at that time for women not to lead and rule? Yes, generally speaking. The answer to this first question suggests that Paul's ban could have been for those days only, but the second question has yet to be asked. **Question B:** Can the underlying principle be expressed equally effectively in some other way? The answer to this, surely, is no, because the law of God plainly bans women from preaching and ruling in the church *(1 Corinthians 14.34)*. There is no question of there being an underlying principle capable of being expressed in a different way, for how can women remain silent in any other way than by remaining silent? It was certainly the case that *culture* required them to remain silent, but the Lord also required them to do so, and there is no alternative way of complying with this command.

Equally, in *1 Timothy 2.12-14* Paul gives a *theological* reason why women may not preach or lead. This makes it clear that while the culture of the day may have demanded this, God demanded it also for important spiritual reasons. Here, then, is a matter far higher than culture. If either of the test questions receives a negative answer it means that the precise form of obedience which is recorded in the Bible is vital. The command can only be obeyed in a literal way.

In the case of the command that Christians should work with their own hands (as craftsmen, perhaps, or labourers), are we all to obey this command in a literal way today? (Paul requires working with hands in *Ephesians 4.28* and *1 Thessalonians 4.11.*) May we not be 'brain' workers? **Question A** asks if the outward form of obedience in those days was a social custom, and the answer is surely yes, for while there were brain workers, the overwhelming majority of people were obliged to work with their hands. **Question B** then asks if the principle underlying the command can be expressed in some other way. What is the underlying principle? It is (says Paul) that we should be able to live honestly, without stealing or scrounging, and also have the means to help others. Can the underlying aims of the command be met by forms of work other than manual work? Of course they can. Times have changed, and the command to live honestly and help others can easily be honoured through desk jobs. Both questions have received an affirmative answer showing that the physical mode of expressing the principle was cultural. (No doubt the relatively few desk workers of Paul's day realised that he expressed this command for the benefit of the masses, and their work also qualified as honest.)

Baptism and the Lord's Supper, however, are examples of activities that were definitely not cultural. If **Question A** is asked – Were these social customs? – the answer would be negative for they were certainly not carried out for the special purpose and in the distinctive way that the Lord required. The baptism of Gentile pros-elytes to the Jewish faith was very different from the baptism of repentance inaugurated by John, and then ordained by Christ. Although it had similarities with Jewish baptism, Christian baptism was a distinctive innovation never carried out before. The Lord's Supper was plainly a deliberate and major change from the Passover supper, with new signs and application. In neither case – baptism or the Lord's Supper – could it be said that the Christian church simply carried on an existing custom. Both ordinances were clearly newly designed for the church of Christ, and so for both the answer to the first question is negative.

Then we put **Question B** – Can the principles underlying Christ's commands be expressed in some other way than that used by the early church? How can they be? How can total washing and death and resurrection be pictured and expressed in any other way than by baptism in water? How can we express eating and drinking the sym-bols of the Lord's body and blood in any other way than by eating and drinking the prescribed bread and wine? In both cases, negative answers to the two questions indicate that there is no cultural alter-native available, and so the ordinances are binding in the very form they were given.

The purpose of this present chapter is not to review a long list of all Christian duties, but solely to establish that the Bible is not a mass of confusion, and that there is no excuse for Christians to give up obedience to its commands. In cases where a duty may be performed in an alternative way to that stated in the Bible (because culture has changed) these simple questions may be asked to establish that this is legitimate. However, Christian teachers who do not want to be closely tied to the Bible pick and choose for them-selves whether something is binding, thus robbing Scripture of its authority.

Should churches appoint elders today, or may they devise their own system of church order? **Question A** asks whether elders of congregations were a social custom? Indeed they were in the synagogues of Jewish society. **Question B** then asks – Can they be replaced in the churches by some other form of office, such as central denominational government, or congregational democracy without officers? Clearly either of the last two possibilities do away with the distinctive role of local elders, so the answer must be negative, in which case the literal prescription of the Bible must be obeyed unaltered.

Take the issue of whether women's head covering is binding for today. This provides a rare example of where Christians may give different answers to the two test questions, but the debatable nature of the issue does not fault the questions. **Question A** asks – Was head covering a social custom? Most will answer in the affirmative; certainly it was the social custom in Corinth, though not everywhere. **Question B** asks – Can the underlying principle be equally expressed in some other way? At this point we encounter disagreement among the most ardent lovers of the Word. Those who answer negatively think that the command is not related to culture, and must be obeyed literally. Others, however, believe that the underlying principle – the need to express modesty and humility – may be expressed differently in other ages and cultures, and that modest feminine deportment should be expressed in the language of dress prevailing in a particular culture.

By providing this example we demonstrate that there will still be some differences of interpretation between those who truly cleave to the Word, but nothing like the state of unworkable confusion talked about by shallow expositors, most of whom simply do not like to be governed by God's Word in the practical affairs of church life.

God has given a wealth of detailed prescriptions in His Word, saying precisely how things should be done in the believer's life and in the churches. His Word is always to be believed, received, and trusted, and any exceptions to the general rule of literal obedience may be easily discerned.

To summarise: all Scripture is binding today unless . . .

1. Scripture itself cancels, limits or modifies what it prescribes.

2. The passage records immoral or irreligious behaviour.

3. An apparent duty appears obscurely in one text only.

4. It can be proved that the thing prescribed may be fully obeyed in different ways in different cultures.

See chart on next page – 'Tests for Whether a New Testament Instruction or Example is to be Literally Obeyed'.

Tests for Whether a New Testament Instruction or Example is to be Literally Obeyed

	QUESTION A: Was the act a social custom?	QUESTION B: Can the underlying principle be equally expressed some other way?
The instruction that we should work with our own hands	YES	YES
The prohibition on women preaching and leading	YES	NO
The washing of feet	YES	YES
Greeting one another with a holy kiss	YES	YES
The Lord's Supper	NO (new)	NO
Baptism	NO (new)	NO
Elders	YES	NO
The financial support of preachers	YES	NO

TWO 'YES' ANSWERS = Culture has shaped the outward expression of the duty. The principle behind the command must be obeyed, but the manner of obeying may change.

ANY 'NO' ANSWERS = The command must be literally obeyed. The *form* of Bible times is the only way to express the principle. It is above culture.

13
Sticking Up for the Judges
A glorious range of heroes denigrated

A PRIME EXAMPLE of a Bible book which has fallen prey to the anti-supernatural processes of the modern approach is the *Book of Judges*, in which deeply spiritual heroes of faith have been horribly maligned and discredited, and the great lessons connected with those heroes of faith lost. Bible dictionaries and commentaries governed by this approach regard *Judges* as a most gloomy book, full of periods of apostasy and woe. They think it illustrates the desperate decline of Israel after the death of Joshua, and the necessity of the monarchy inaugurated under Saul. The key-note of the book is said to be the sad sentence of the last verse – 'In those days there was no king in Israel: every man did that which was right in his own eyes.' What a miserable history of darkness and anarchy it is, recorded only to prove that the people needed a king!

The problem with this idea is that the giving of a king was *not* what God intended for His people, for it is repeatedly described in Scripture as a downward step. Samuel warned Israel against a monarchy, and spelled out to the people how it would turn out to be a source of misery, and so it proved to be. The *Book of Judges* would hardly be intended by God to justify something which was wrong, and which would give even greater trouble. A simple piece of arithmetic shows that the Israelites fared better in the time of the judges than they did under kings. The narrative speaks of 111 years of oppression compared with 286 years of peace and quietness, under the mild and non-bureaucratic rule of the judges, an overwhelming ratio of peace to trouble. During the monarchy, however (taking account of both the kings of Judah and Israel), the position was far worse because bad kings outnumbered good kings, and times of insecurity and captivity outnumbered times of peace and liberty by more than three-to-one.

The time of the judges was far superior in many ways to the period of the monarchy. It was certainly not, as some have said, a time untouched by spiritual understanding, and characterised throughout by anarchy and moral ignorance. How can modern approach writers paint such a dismal picture of a period which saw triumphs of such magnitude that four judges secured a place in the *Hebrews 11* hall of fame? One reason is the fatal rule of the modern approach that no Scripture passage written subsequently should be allowed to throw light on an earlier passage because the earlier author would not have known about it.

As we have said before, we believe that the entire Bible was written in eternity past by a single author, namely Christ, and if He provides a commentary on *Judges* in the New Testament, we had better make use of it.

It is true that each period of peace in the *Book of Judges* deteriorates into sin and punishment in a series of cycles. It is also true that the final chapters describe a period of horrific evil, but these events undoubtedly occurred at the beginning of the time of the judges, as the record shows (and as we demonstrate in Appendix II on page 157). Nevertheless, there are also seasons of deep repentance, culminating in great blessing as judges were given by God and inspired to demonstrate the power of faith and obedience, and to prefigure a future great Deliverer. These judges were *saviours*, governors and magistrates. Matthew Poole tells us they were – 'inferiors to kings, and could neither make new laws, nor impose any tributes, but were the supreme executors of *God's* laws and commands'.

While they ruled, the land was as close as it could be to pure theocracy, for there was no dictator and no ruler aside from God. And while the Ark of the Covenant remained in Shiloh, the power of God stood by them, ready to bless.

The gloomy view of the judges turns out, on inspection, to be entirely superficial. It is easy to ascribe bad motives to these deliverers and to 'discover' deficiencies in them, but if the rule of interpretation adopted is that of *Hebrews 11* (contrary to the modern approach), then we look more carefully, realising and remembering that they were great men of faith, and our minds are cleared to see the record in quite another light.

What, then, are we to make of the judges? How we see them will determine our understanding of everything that takes place, and whether or not we find the inherent spiritual lessons for today. For the interpreter there is a choice to be made between the following two lists. On the one hand we may regard them as –

- regenerate and spiritual
- holy and faithful
- people with a spiritual mission
- people who saw the all-important issue to be the spiritual kingdom of Heaven and not just the earthly prosperity of the Jews.

On the other hand, we may regard them as –

- people of their age
- not necessarily regenerate
- prone to use unworthy methods

- frequently sinful and irresponsible
- lacking the light and understanding of men like Abraham and Moses
- people who brought only earthly deliverance to the Jews.

First, we will briefly prove that the judges *must* be regarded in the first manner – as *spiritually enlightened* people. Then we will review the spiritual lessons coming from this view – magnificent applications to the lives of believers, unavailable to those who take a negative view of the judges. The first list is the more traditional view of Bible interpretation, the view of the overwhelming majority of preachers since the Reformation until modern times, when it has been put aside under liberal influence.

To prove the spirituality of the judges we refer again to that great chapter of faith, *Hebrews 11*, which tells us that key judges must be viewed as spiritually enlightened people, a quality doubtless shared by all of them. The four named judges (Gideon, Barak, Samson and Jephthah) are severely criticised in modern evangelical books, but the verdict of God is that they were great stalwarts of faith.

They believed in a heavenly future

Hebrews 11.39 makes it clear that all named in the chapter are *commended by God for their faith.* What kind of faith did they have? Was it only reliance on God to solve some pressing military crisis? Not according to *Hebrews*, where it is commended as being faith in God's righteous covenant, faith in God's promises, and even faith in a future resurrection.

> 'And what shall I more say? for the time would fail me to tell of Gedeon, and of Barak, and of Samson, and of Jephthae; of David also, and Samuel, and of the prophets: who through faith subdued kingdoms, wrought righteousness, obtained promises . . . that they might obtain a better resurrection' *(Hebrews 11.32-35).*

Hebrews 11 is all about *spiritual* faith, and the key judges are there linked with the patriarchs before them, and with David and the prophets after them. In heart and mind they were not of this world, but set their ultimate aims and affections on heavenly things. We repeat that the judges appear in a glorious list of people who believed in future, unseen blessings, being of the same spiritual calibre as Abel, Enoch, Noah, Abraham, Sara, Isaac, Jacob, Joseph, Moses and Rahab.

Nothing destroys the *Book of Judges* more than to turn these heroes of faith into civil and military devotees of an earthly state who were only zealous for the *earthly* prosperity of the people, and who understood little of the true way of salvation; yet that is exactly what the modern approach does. The judges were certainly ready to obey whenever God moved them to deliver the people, but they also realised that the only real hope for the souls of people was salvation, and the future to which they most looked forward was a heavenly one. We must see the New Testament in the Old to understand their theology and motivation, and *Hebrews 11* is our essential 'commentary'.

We should not be greatly surprised to learn of the spiritually enlightened status of the judges because all the light of the Pentateuch, not to mention the *Book of Joshua*, was available to them. They possessed a powerful heritage of doctrine. They stood in an intensely self-conscious cultural tradition, and in possession of the law and the covenant. The idea that there was an unbridged gap in spiritual knowledge between the death of Joshua and the beginning of the monarchy is not credible. The judges would have known what Abraham felt about the promises of God, and that he did not go about to establish an earthly kingdom, but lived in tents and looked for a heavenly one. They surely knew that he had been a stranger and pilgrim on the earth whose heart was set on a divine fulfilment of the promises made to him. They knew the words of God to Moses

(*Exodus 3.6*) – 'I am the God of thy father, the God of Abraham, the God of Isaac, and the God of Jacob' – implying that these were presently alive with Him.

The judges also had the record of Jacob's dream at Bethel, showing interaction between Heaven and earth, a scene which led Jacob to call that place the gate of Heaven. Further back, they had the record of Enoch, translated directly by God to be with Him in Heaven. The Scriptures made the judges aware that God's purposes went far beyond and above their earthly and national circumstances.

They saw divine appearances

There are powerful indications of the spiritually enlightened status of the judges within the book itself, the first being the occurrence of theophanies, by which Christ appeared and spoke to them. This would obviously have confirmed their realisation that they dealt with a living God Who could be personally known, and would have encouraged them for the rest of their lives to serve 'as seeing him who is invisible'. *Judges* is a book of theophanies, and we can scarcely imagine the powerful effect that these must have had on the convictions of those who were blessed by them. At times they must have felt as though they were in the vestibule of Heaven, dramatically sensing the eternal context of their lives. Theophanies demonstrated mightily that they were engaged on a spiritual mission for a living and eternal Lord.

They sought no kingly honours

A further indication of the enlightened spirituality of the judges is drawn from their disregard for worldly honours, for not one of them would allow himself to be made a king. They did not seek such a position, and when supreme office was offered to them it was declined. They neither pursued nor acquired privileges such as a noble court, a retinue of servants, bodyguards, or royal succession for their children, but they limited themselves to the pattern permitted by the Lord for those days. They were men of clear obedience to the system left in the books of Moses and Joshua, which made no provision for a monarchy. They served the King of Heaven, Who alone was the royal ruler of His people.

The lessons of Judges

Chapter one sets the scene and we are introduced at once to a great change in the fortunes of the children of Israel, providing a spiritual parallel to the experience of the church in our day. In the early verses, two of their tribes easily overpower a pagan king who had himself defeated seventy warrior-kings, cutting off his big toes and thumbs just as he had done to defeated foes to prevent them from successfully wielding swords or riding war-horses again. At this stage two tribes could capture the subduer of seventy kings, whereas by verse 19 Judah could achieve only a partial victory, due to their spiritual compromise and forfeiture of God's blessing. We are told that – 'when Israel was strong . . . they put the Canaanites to tribute, and did not utterly drive them out' (verse 28). When she was strong she could have put the Canaanites out of the land, but instead took revenue from them, and when she became weak they overran her.

The story of many churches over recent decades is one of failure to work vigorously for the Gospel, until the day arrives when they shrink to near invisibility in their communities, and no longer have the strength to grasp opportunities. A low level of evangelistic activity, coupled with borrowing from surrounding worldly culture in worship and lifestyle, is prefigured in the experience of Israel at the beginning of the *Book of Judges*.

Chapter two reflects another feature of present-day evangelical life, namely, the ability to feel strongly about certain things without doing much about them. The Angel of the Lord preached to the people with the result that they were deeply convicted of their failure, and began to weep terribly. They wept so much, so long, and so hard that the very name of the place was changed to 'Weepers'. Unfortunately, the weeping made no lasting difference, demonstrating that sorrow over sin or over duties omitted does not necessarily lead to remedial action. We all know of people who have made an art form of washing away pangs of conviction by tears, rather than by change of conduct. We may weep for awakening, but does it improve the evangelistic work rate of the church?

The first judge to be considered by name appears in chapter three, when an eight-year period of bondage is terminated by Othniel, who secures a forty-year peace. The two main offences giving rise to God's punishment had been intermarriage with Canaanites, and spiritual compromise. These were the principal recurring offences in the period of the judges, as well as throughout the subsequent monarchy. The worldliness of today's evangelicalism is again prefigured, particularly in bringing the idiom of this world into worship and evangelism.

Also in chapter three is the account of Ehud, who ended eighteen years of oppression by plunging a dagger into the stomach of the Moabite king. Ehud worked alone, probably because the people had grown too weak and cowardly. The Lord often uses individuals to revive His cause in days of great weakness when the majority of believers have become indifferent and inactive. Ehud was a divinely appointed instrument, and not, as modern commentaries say, a person of questionable morals who 'stooped to assassination'. His nation was at war, his act very courageous, and we are bound to assume that he acted under divine direction.

Judges chapter four brings the reader to Deborah and Barak, people who should be highly esteemed, and all the more so in the light of *Hebrews 11*, where Barak is named as a hero of faith. Surprisingly, he is often portrayed as a cringing, cowardly individual who needed reproof from Deborah before undertaking his mission. However, because his strong spiritual trust is confirmed to us in *Hebrews*, we are bound to draw the following conclusions about the events involving him. After twenty years of oppression the prophetess Deborah received the command of God to march upon the oppressor, and she transmitted that command to Barak. The Lord had said to Deborah that the enemy commander would be driven into their hands. Barak does not hesitate, but he is neither a judge nor a prophet at this point, and if he acts, how shall it be seen that this is the Lord's doing, not his own, and how shall the glory be the Lord's when victory is won? If the prophetess is involved, then he can be sure that events will be rightly interpreted by the people, and all the glory will be given to the Lord.

As though to confirm that this was Barak's concern, Deborah assures him that his leadership will not bring him personal glory, but that the execution of the enemy general will be given to an obscure woman. Barak's mind being at peace, he carries out his mission with immense courage, and the eventual victory leads to forty years of peace. His avoidance of personal glory in favour of God's glory is one of the lessons of the passage applicable to pastors in our day.

The nature of the victory is another great lesson, for we see human effort greatly magnified by divine intervention as God sends a fearful night storm to swell the river the enemy must cross, so that a raging torrent sweeps their chariots away. We learn from this that God's method is often to greatly magnify the efforts of His people, and we certainly need this lesson today. The Lord wonderfully uses human instruments, but, to be used, they must do something.

To see these lessons is not to make use of the Bible as a source of imaginatively devised illustration. In the light of the expectations given to us in the New Testament, we believe that the *Judges* record is intended to yield such parallels and lessons. The way God works does not change, and so He will respond to us as He responded to these people of old. The world does not change either, nor human nature. This record is for our reproof, correction, stimulation and encouragement.

Judges chapter five – a song of praise and gratitude – establishes beyond doubt the forwardness of *both* Deborah and Barak. The leaders led and the people volunteered, and Deborah sings of the great willingness of the governors (including Barak). There is so much in this song which should be channelled into pastoral application today, principally the message that without earnest enthusiasm, much practical effort, and courageous faith, little can be achieved for the Lord. But there are also strong notes of condemnation in this song for those who were unwilling to serve.

The tribe of Reuben is mentioned, whose people talked much about going to war, but took no action. Here is an obvious application to our present climate when many will debate and discuss the theology of revival, and rightly promote prayer for it, but so few are inclined to act and preach evangelistically.

Gilead also kept out of the way, and Dan preferred commercial business to the service of God. The inhabitants of the town of Meroz are especially cursed for not coming to the help of the cause of God. It is a terrible thought that in every congregation there are always some who possess spiritual blessings and abilities but who never come to the help of the work, avoiding the trials and labours of service. Perhaps they need a glimpse of the Lord's displeasure in the curse of Meroz.

Evangelical writers following the modern approach deal high-handedly with Jael, who killed Sisera. They accuse her of coarse brutality, but if they considered Deborah's inspired song, they would see Jael praised and applauded above other women. They are cruelly wrong, as usual, for she was undoubtedly a sensitive, gentle, godly woman who did something utterly abhorrent to her, but did it because she clearly knew the prophecy that a woman's hand would fell the enemy general.

The application is plain – the believer may sometimes have a duty to do something extremely hard, even against his natural disposition and inclination, but the Lord will give strength. So, surely, Jael closed her eyes and cried out to God to enable her to carry out the predicted act against all her sensitivities, for if God had spoken, it must be done.

Judges chapter six is about Gideon and the appearance of the Lord to him. Once again we have to decide between two starkly contrasting interpretations. It is said that Gideon was a faithless man who repeatedly asked for signs. One writer cynically says that when the Lord greeted him with the high praise, 'the Lord is with thee, thou mighty man of valour', the words were spoken in sarcasm, or at the very least with teasing humour. The right interpretation begins with the *Hebrews 11* key, identifying Gideon as a spiritual man already equipped with great trust in the Lord. This view takes the Lord's greeting seriously, as an indication that Gideon could be used because of his great faith and courage.

Gideon had distinguished himself already, probably as an effective resistance worker providing food for the oppressed Israelites. He knew very well that the people had sinned and failed, and said, in effect, 'Oh Lord, with all this tragedy, surely we have now been permanently rejected.' His spiritual insight was commended, for he understood that God must punish sin. It was this light, combined with faith and frustration at the lack of action, which was his 'might', which the Lord would use. For us today, Gideon pictures believers who feel ashamed of their inactivity, and are grieved at the victory of worldliness over the Gospel. It is people who feel like this who are usable by the Lord.

When Gideon pointed out that he lacked the means to accomplish the defeat of the Midianites, he was not complaining but seeking help and direction. We know this from his commendation as a man of faith in *Hebrews.* How could such a person as he save Israel? His family was poor and he wielded no noble authority. How could he even raise a sufficiently powerful force from such a demoralised people? His questions were realistic and reasonable, and the Lord assured him that He would work through him, and empower him.

Gideon asked for a sign, a request which indicated his humility rather than his lack of faith. Before plunging Israelites into a war that could bring terrible reprisals, he needed to be sure that he rightly understood the Lord's command, and that he was not acting on personal impulse. So today, the aspiring preacher should be ready to test his call in a spiritual way, and not to plunge ahead without clear attestation. A congregation should be willing to search the Scriptures, rather than blindly accept any and every proposed gimmick that comes along.

If we view Gideon in the light of *Hebrews 11* we have vital applications to believers today, but if we accept the modern approach, refusing to let so-called 'later' texts inform the passage, we forfeit those pastoral applications. As the wonder of a theophany dawned on Gideon, he felt under judgement in the presence of God, and, for all his human valour, we see also humility and godly fear. If only we also could combine courage and confidence in the Lord with a *lack* of self-confidence and a deep awareness of our need of grace, then we would have the balance of a Gideon.

Subsequently, God moved Gideon to burn his father's altar to Baal, plunging his mission into a storm of antagonism and opposition. His own family as well as all the townspeople now wanted him sentenced to death. He had no money, and his nation was away from God, demoralised by oppressors. But despite the impossible circumstances, he believed the promises of God, and prepared to carry out the task God had given him. Why then, if he was so trusting, did he ask for yet further assurance from God? Why was there a *double* trial of God in the incident of the fleece?

We remember once again that Gideon was about to risk thousands of lives through offering armed resistance, and if he were deluded in his understanding of God's will, a most terrible humiliation of his nation and its testimony could occur. He had to be certain that the Lord was truly sending him on this seemingly unachievable assignment, and it was in that spirit that he asked for such extensive tokens.

We have great advantages over Gideon in these days, for we already have all the assurances we need in the record and promises of the Word of God, as well as in the history of the church, that God is with His witnessing people. We have the example of the New Testament, of the early church, and of periods of reformation, martyrdom, and awakening. We have more fleeces than we could desire to give us liberated faith in the power of God. We will never have to ask for a special sign like Gideon, a great hero of faith who nevertheless had only six books of the Bible (by present day reckoning). But like him we must make certain that all our activities for the Lord are carried out in the way He has commanded. Modern evangelicalism fails at this point, with its overconfidence and self-reliance.

In *Judges* chapter seven we read of the massive army, but 22,000 men were rejected from the outset. Here is yet more evidence of the great courage and faith of Gideon, for we can scarcely imagine a man of little faith immediately sending all those men home.

After the rejection of 22,000, another 9,700 had to be pruned out, and eventually only 300 were left. There are different explanations for Gideon's water-lapping test of *Judges 7.5*, but a most acceptable verdict seems to be that this was a way of identifying true worshippers. Baal worship involved much kneeling and bending of the head to the ground, and this posture had therefore assumed offensive significance to those who were truly spiritual. Kneeling smacked so strongly of Baal worship that the godly could not drop to their knees and bend their heads to the water. Probably they squatted or stooped and used cupped hands, lapping the water out of their hands. Gideon was moved to use only the godly for the Lord's work. There is another lesson here for would-be evangelists who depend on the help and co-operation of non-evangelicals, together with crowd-effect, emotional hysteria, spectacular 'healings' and huge budgets to accomplish the rescue of sinners from the world. In Gideon's campaign the 'arm of flesh' was sent home.

A special pastoral application of this event is drawn from the fact that only 300 men were used. The Midianite oppression was among the very worst, being conspicuously vicious and barbaric, yet the smallest army was selected to overthrow them. We remember that before the Reformation there were only a few contenders for the Truth placed here and there, such as John Wycliffe and his poor preachers, a mere handful, and yet tremendous instrumentality was theirs. The Reformation began with one monk nailing his ninety-five theses to the door of the castle church at Wittenberg in 1517.

A little over two centuries later, in 1739, a cold, grey dawn witnessed a relatively small band of believers gathered on a London common round a young, squinting preacher named George Whitefield, but that was the beginning of an awakening which rocked London, and the entire country. Today, when we are surrounded by cities larger than history has ever seen, and minds are bombarded by an intensely atheistic media, believers feel like tiny hopeless specks in the midst of a faceless humanity. We are strengthened by the thought that Gideon's minute army succeeded, because it is the Lord's strange work to manifest His power through small groups of committed people, amplifying their every effort. If revival came today, it could be that thousands of surprised believers might be disqualified from instrumentality because of their uncommitted lives. Soundness by itself is not enough.

The men of Ephraim, who had been least affected by the oppression, complained bitterly that they had not been called to take part in the action against the Midianites, but they had taken no initiative to help the remainder of the land. Their complacency was all the more inexcusable as they were the principal tribe and enjoyed the prestige of having the most important religious towns, Bethel and Shiloh, within their borders. By way of application, Ephraim could almost be seen to represent the evangelical *establishment,* or possibly settled churches which enjoy great comfort and fail to take real initiatives for the furtherance of the cause of the cross.

Gideon had not called the Ephraimites because God did not want them. They were lazy and unconcerned until they suffered a loss of 'face' or reputation. It is interesting that all Gideon had to do to placate them was to make mention of their past battle honours. The thought that they were still respected for bygone deeds seemed to satisfy them. How many churches, preachers, and individual believers are more concerned about what people think of them than what they are currently achieving for the Lord?

Judges chapter eight includes verses showing Gideon rejecting the offer of kingly status. However, although he had stood as a true hero of faith, there arose a tragic inconsistency in Gideon's life which led to great heartache for his family and for the land, and the inspired record does not spare him so that pastoral lessons can be drawn in subsequent days. He acquired numerous wives. The sorry narrative of chapter nine shows how polygamy threw open the door to a whirlwind of murder and rebellion, seventy sons being murdered by one. The record stands as a warning of the consequences of failing to honour the Lord's command *in all things.*

In our time the near total collapse of the 'royal house' of evangelicalism in Britain has been through the unbelief and the actions of 'illegitimate' sons within the household, who have murdered by compromising the faith and bringing in worldliness, poisoning churches and grieving away the Spirit. It has been too easy for people lacking a genuine conversion experience to join the membership of churches. Surely such warnings as this are among the vital lessons of these historical narratives.

Later, when the children of Israel had again turned to the gods of the surrounding nations, the Philistines and Ammonites were allowed by God to oppress them for eighteen years. Jephthah, another hero of faith in *Hebrews 11*, was expelled from his home and heritage by his brothers. He went into the land of Tob (probably Ish-tob of *2 Samuel 10.6*) outside Israelite territory, to become the leader of a group of bankrupts whose fallen fortunes encouraged them to respond against the oppressors of their nation. (The word translated 'vain' in *Judges 11.3* literally means *emptied* or *worthless*, indicating people who were dispossessed.)

Jephthah is commended from the beginning of the narrative for might and valour, and is the obvious choice of general in the mind of the Gilead elders to repel the Ammonites. It is most probable that he was already valiantly fighting the Lord's battles. His many daring exploits and skirmishes against Israel's oppressor were plainly the activities of a man of God, not the activities of a common brigand. (How differently we look at such a life when we take seriously the *Hebrews 11* comments!)

Jephthah demanded greater honesty and sincerity from the Israelites before he agreed to their request to lead them. Several lessons may be distinguished for us today. First, when the people cried out for the restoration of their past they were not immediately granted deliverance. So today, we cannot expect a restoration of evangelical blessing at the mere asking. How earnest are we? How truly do we desire change? How ready are we to work for it? How ready are we to obey *all* the commands of the Word?

There could be no answer to prayer for the Israelites until foreign gods were actually put away. Will present-day believers empty their homes of the gods of excessive materialism which have robbed the work of God for so many years? And once again we ask: will we abandon the worldly worship forms so beloved in numerous churches?

There could be no deliverance for the Israelites until they were ready to act in a zealous, costly and courageous manner. Jephthah was already putting them to shame, albeit with a small band of men who had no other income but the spoils which they recovered. Only when the children of Israel recognised the Lord's servant, and were ready to follow him into battle, were they delivered. So today, only when comfortable Christians begin to stand behind their preachers and follow them into new levels of zealous activity for the Lord, will there be a return of evangelical power. The sad lament of pastors who cannot get their people to operate Sunday Schools must become a thing of the past, if prayer is to be heard. All these things, Paul tells us, were written for our learning, and the expounder must discern the spiritual and moral application intended for the people of God today.

In *Judges* chapter eleven there is the vexed matter of Jephthah's vow to the Lord –

> 'Whatsoever cometh forth of the doors of my house to meet me, when I return in peace from the children of Ammon, shall surely be the Lord's, and I will offer it up for a burnt offering.'

Victory is given to him and when he returns it is his only daughter who first emerges from his house to meet him. Now it is plain that when Jephthah made his vow, he might have expected the welcome of his family, and it is unthinkable that he vowed to burn one of them. Here is a good example of how the interpretation of a passage is affected by how one estimates the judge in question. Some modern commentators have no respect for the spirituality of this judge, insisting that one act after another was not according to Christian standards. But if we are guided by the *Hebrews 11* key, we cannot conceive that Jephthah, a man with a spiritual outlook, would have been no better than the Ammonites whom God had just enabled him to defeat. He clearly stood for the right way, as opposed to the wrong way.

We may safely assume that Jephthah intended that the person to greet him would be consecrated to the Lord along the lines of the Nazarite vow practised in those days. Under this vow, his daughter would be dedicated to God not to marry and bear children, and the line of Jephthah would die out. Her wonderful and gracious response includes a request that she might spend two months visiting all her friends to 'bewail my virginity' before her consecration to the vow. This would be a strange thing to bewail if it had not been the subject of the vow.

To confirm the interpretation, when Scripture records the performing of the vow it says that Jephthah 'did with her according to his vow which he had vowed: and she knew no man'. This phrase surely signifies the *nature* of the vow, namely the consecration of the daughter to virginity. Some think that the annual four-day lamentation which was observed by the women of the land points to her having been sacrificed. But Jephthah would have inaugurated the observance for positive reasons, so that for four days in the year her example of consecration to the Lord in thanksgiving for victory would be remembered. Whatever we may think of such a demanding vow today, we learn that a costly sacrifice of dedication in recognition of special blessing and instrumentality seemed to Jephthah a natural obligation and offering.

What offering will we give for the privilege of great answers to prayer, for our loved ones perhaps, or for souls saved through our ministries? For greater blessing, will we give greater earnestness, and more costly stewardship, and more fervent devotion? We cannot pay for our instrumentality or benefits, but we should certainly yield and render something for the kindness of the Lord.

In *Judges* chapter twelve the men of Ephraim gather themselves together to challenge Jephthah, just as they had challenged Gideon before him. As ever, they had taken no initiative in the offensive, made no contribution, and so the Lord had had no use for them. But in their own estimation they were the people who mattered, and they were insulted at having been passed over. Indolent and jealous, they thought they had a right to be consulted about how things would be done and, unhappily, they have their counterparts in many churches today. So the Ephraimites began to speak against the Gileadites with taunts and insults, and eventually there was war.

To this day those who will not act in the cause of Christ spend much energy speaking against those who will. But the Lord is gracious, and if His obedient, serving people continue in His cause, committing all their problems to Him in prayer, then who knows but that the Lord may deliver them from such problems and impediments, as He ultimately delivered Jephthah.

Even the recurring phases of downgrade and oppression in *Judges* speak to us today. In times of reformation and revival one could think that the devil and atheism had been defeated, but in due course they will rear their heads again. Many churches at the end of the nineteenth century, and in the twentieth, separated themselves from theological liberalism to stand for Truth, but tragically, in time, some of these were taken over by compromise and error. Every age faces a different manifestation of unbelief and false teaching, but God will bless and protect those who are vigilant and faithful in the battle. So many lessons and encouragements flow from the profound history of *Judges*.

14

The Enigma of Samson
A later text solves the problem

OW SHOULD we view the life and exploits of Samson, in view of the almost universal opinion of modern approach evangelical writers that he was a headstrong, erratic character driven by carnal instinct and lust? If we prefer to take the conflicting *Hebrews 11* classification of him as a hero of faith and a spiritual man, how will this shape our perception of his seemingly wayward deeds?

The life of Samson begins in *Judges 13*, where we read of a forty-year period of oppression by the Philistines. We note that Samson's activities did not end the oppression of the Philistines, and in this he was unusual for a deliverer-judge. He greatly troubled and subdued the oppressors, but never entirely overwhelmed them. In *Judges 13.5* the Angel of the Lord prophesied that he would be instrumental in *beginning* the deliverance, not in wholly achieving it.

Samson judged Israel in the days of the Philistines for twenty years, his period of judgeship fitting into the latter part of the forty-year-long oppression and largely overlapping that of Samuel

(Samson judging in the south-west of the land and Samuel more in the centre). Samson's final act, the destruction of the Temple of Dagon, at Gaza, occurred shortly before the Battle of Mizpeh (*1 Samuel 7*).

Samson's great acts of faith were performed without an army because the people were in such a state of spiritual degradation and idolatrous compromise that God would not use them. However, through Samson, the Lord demonstrated what was possible if only they would repent and trust Him. If God's representative could do such things unaided by the people, how much more could they do together if they returned to the Lord. Yet they did not repent until Mizpeh.

Judges 13 records the appearance of the Angel of the Lord to Samson's parents, clearly a pre-incarnate appearance of Christ, as the rule of *John 1.18* applies throughout time – 'No man hath seen God at any time; the only begotten Son, which is in the bosom of the Father, he hath declared him.' Samson's mother perceived the Lord only as a 'man of God', and likewise his father did not realise that this was the 'angel of the Lord'. The 'man of God' directed that an offering be offered 'unto the Lord', and declared His name to be 'secret', or rather – 'beyond understanding, mysterious and wonderful'. When He ascended to the skies in the flame of the altar, then both husband and wife knew that they had 'seen God', and believed that He would begin to deliver Israel out of the hand of the Philistines by their child.

The record tells us that the Lord blessed Samson as he grew, and at manhood began to move him by the Spirit. But in spite of the directions given in *Hebrews 11* that he is to be viewed as a man of faith, modern evangelical knives are out for Samson as soon as his ministry begins. One leading evangelical commentator says that 'his life seems to have revolved around illicit relationships with prostitutes and loose-living women.' He is viewed as a failure and a spiritual anarchist. It is even said that his exploits 'read like the actions of an uncontrollable juvenile delinquent'. The only useful application of Samson's life suggested by a popular Bible dictionary is that God is showing us He is prepared to use some very unsatisfactory instruments in His service. This kind of application could well be an encouragement to slack Christian living.

A leading evangelical Bible handbook speaks of his 'selfish, sensual and irresponsible behaviour'. The same book goes on to ask, 'How can people like these be commended for their faith? How could God use them? There is no satisfactory answer to questions like these.' Of course there is no answer if our chosen method of interpretation is the modern approach, for then all useful pastoral application is swept away.

Using the interpretive key of *Hebrews 11*, and the clear statement of God in *Judges 13* that He would use Samson as His representative, we advance to *Judges 14*, where Samson desired to marry a Philistine woman. His parents anxiously remonstrated with him, but the *Judges* narrative states clearly that Samson's initiative was 'of the Lord'. Although he did not share the reason with his parents, we are told that the Lord intended him to find just cause to take action against the Philistines. Presumably, therefore, Samson acted by faith, in response to divine direction, and not out of carnal lust.

But why should his parents have been left out of the 'plot'? Needless to say Samson is rebuked by modern evangelical writers for lack of submission to his parents, and for his allegedly curt, rude dismissal of their protests, while being overwhelmed by 'wretched lust'. In the light of his being a man of faith, following God's direction, it is rather more likely that he sought to deliver them from great anxiety.

Most modern exegetes pounce on the unlawfulness of Samson marrying a Philistine, but older writers point out that the law of *Deuteronomy 7.1-5* did not specifically mention marriage to a

Philistine, and (more realistically) that the law had a reason attached to it, namely that the ban on Canaanite marriages was to avoid idolatry. Samson, however, knew from the Lord that his marriage would result in a blow being struck against idolatry. It has also been pointed out by old writers that *Deuteronomy 7.1-5* is *ceremonial* law, rather than *moral* law, which God could legitimately set aside for the carrying out of His purposes. Yet another explanation suggests that Samson knew from the Lord that the marriage would never be consummated on account of the treachery of the Philistines, and this was certainly how events turned out.

The wealth of material from past commentators (acting under the direction of *Hebrews 11*) is of far greater quality and depth than that offered by followers of the modern approach. The older exegetes compared Scripture with Scripture, and by this they were aware of a parallel between Samson's marriage and the offering up of Isaac. Abraham, in faith, obeyed God, believing that if He commanded it, there could be no murder, concluding that the Lord intended to raise Isaac up again. Likewise Samson, by faith, obeyed the guidance of God which had come to him so very clearly. He realised that God was going to do something through the arranging of this marriage, because God would not lead him into sin. Milton (in the drama of *Samson Agonistes*) gives Samson the following words:

> The first I saw at Timna, and she pleased
> Me, not my parents, that I sought to wed
> The daughter of an infidel: they knew not
> That what I motioned was of God; I knew
> From intimate impulse, and therefore urged
> The marriage on; that by occasion hence
> I might begin Israel's deliverance,
> The work to which I was divinely called.

God, it transpired, was guiding Samson to do something which would make him a target for the vindictive conduct of the oppressing Philistines. If he were to perform the role of a one-man army against vicious enemy occupation, then he must personally suffer a degree of murderous antagonism which would justify his response. The overbearing conduct of the enemy Philistines had reached grotesque proportions, descending to the worst standards of oppression. In such days an oppressor would trade with the oppressed and never pay. If the injured party protested, they would torch their fields and houses. So the Philistines played cruel games with the Israelite population, tantalising, teasing and hurting them constantly. They made sport of them, doing their utmost to afflict, debase and further crush this already subjugated people.

When Samson married a Philistine woman their response was entirely predictable. First they would humour him, and then cheat him, but by their own law Samson would have just cause to retaliate. The case of the famous riddle provoked the first wave of deceit and fraud from thirty young Philistine guests, who threatened Samson's bride and her household with death if she did not procure the solution for them. The Spirit of the Lord empowered Samson to punish the Philistines, and we may be sure that God, Who does all things well, caused His judgement to fall on people as wicked as the murderous wedding crowd. When Samson was under the control of the Spirit of God, we may be certain his anger was a righteous anger.

Samson's bride was given to his Philistine best man, a certain indication of the non-consummation of the marriage, and proof that the Philistines for their part had never intended that the wedding ceremony would be honoured. However, the marriage would serve to expose more of the cruel and dishonest behaviour of the Philistines.

In *Judges 15* Samson was constrained to visit his bride, ostensibly to attempt a completion of the marriage, but her father resisted him, saying she had been given to another husband. Having had his rightful wife stolen, Samson was moved (and entitled) to punish the local Philistines with the destruction of their crops. It should be remembered that Philistines had doubtless ravaged the fields of the Israelites countless times during the long years of oppression. The Philistines responded by killing Samson's bride and her father, so becoming guilty of murdering his 'family', and giving him (by their own law and customs) the right to judge them.

All this was surely allowed by God to prove to the Israelites that no dealings with the Philistines would ever be honoured by them. The Israelites thought their oppressor was invincible, and servile ingratiation was the only policy. Through Samson the Philistines were shown to be neither invincible nor trustworthy. So it is today, as far as churches are concerned. Many churches think that worldliness cannot be resisted, and that partial, 'managed' acceptance is the only way to survive. In come the rock bands with slightly sanctified worldly music, for how else, they say, can young people be attracted or retained? So-called traditionalists or conservatives who disagree with this policy are seen as a nuisance, but this was exactly the case with Samson. The cowardly Israelites could not see that the Philistines' oppression would never mellow, and their destructive cruelties would never end. Churches today need to grasp that the god of this world, once inside the churches, will do everything necessary to bring them down.

The next move was from the Philistines who hunted down Samson with a great force, the terrified Israelites pleading with him to allow them to hand him over as a prisoner. 'Knowest thou not,' they said, 'that the Philistines are rulers over us?' As far as the servile Israelites were concerned, this was the way it was bound to continue. Not even Samson's exploits could bring them to believe in the availability of God's power, should they trust Him and burn their idols. How low they had fallen to plead with their deliverer to give away his life, and leave them in idolatry and oppression!

Yet it happens today in many places where faithful pastors plead for a return to wholehearted commitment to the Lord's work, and the people of God shy away. We know of pastors who cannot raise so much as a handful of members to re-open a defunct Sunday School, or persuade elders and deacons to resist new-style worship experiments. Is this not the same faithless syndrome seen in the children of Israel long ago? These things were written for our learning and our admonition.

Samson, however, was a hero of faith who knew that God would use him to punish and restrain the Philistines. It is by a remarkable and certainly a spiritual faith that he allowed himself to be bound and handed over to those who intended to kill him. Was this the conduct of a faithless scoundrel? As a prisoner about to be illegally executed he was fully justified in slaying the entire enemy contingent, and the Spirit of the Lord came mightily upon him to rout the oppressors *(Judges 15.14)*.

Two important matters are clear at this point of the narrative. Firstly, contrary to the opinions of fault-finding exegetes, Samson had not yet been motivated by unworthy passions or selfish, irresponsible desires. The inspired record indicates no divine disapproval. It is evident that this warrior-judge had been entirely guided by God to put himself in the way of Philistine oppression, and that every step had been attended by the Holy Spirit. Secondly, he had acted, on every occasion of conflict, with immense courage and faith.

Evidence of Samson's supposedly petulant, self-gratifying nature is seen by his detractors in his conduct after the slaying of the Philistine host with the jawbone of an ass *(Judges 15.15)*. The record says:

> 'He was sore athirst, and called on the Lord, and said, Thou hast given this great deliverance into the hand of thy servant: and now shall I die for thirst, and fall into the hand of the uncircumcised?'

But there is no reason to see peevishness in this prayer unless one has already made up one's mind that Samson was a bad character. Again, with the *Hebrews* hall of fame in mind, we read the prayer entirely differently, allowing for considerable exhaustion in Samson commensurate with having fought a mighty army single-handedly. We note his thanksgiving to God, despite his pain and fatigue, giving all the glory to Him for victory. We then see a real fear, not so much that his exhaustion would consume him, but that the Philistines would pluck victory out of defeat by his death, and the cause of the Lord be defamed. His much maligned prayer unites gratitude with a cry for future help, in the spirit of Newton's lines –

> *He that hath led me hitherto*
> *Shall lead me all my journey through.*

A curious statement comes at the end of *Judges 15*. It is recorded that Samson 'judged Israel in the days of the Philistines twenty years'. It is strange to see this at this point of the narrative because the life of Samson was not yet over. It is an early obituary, prematurely placed to show that for most of his life Samson was a true and worthy judge, but also to mark the point at which he fell from his faithfulness and privileged instrumentality. The sad, final part of his life is placed virtually in an appendix.

From this point blemishes appear in his conduct as he visits Gaza and stays with 'an harlot', although some older commentators stoutly maintain that he only *lodged* with this 'society courtesan'. It is just possible that his moral fall did not occur immediately. The fact that he went alone to Gaza, the chief fortified city of the Philistines, shows that his heroism and victories had significantly subdued them. Did he go to walk the city streets just to remind them of his presence and might?

Evidence that Samson went to Gaza on a divine mission, but fell into sin during the course of it, is seen in that God did not immediately abandon him, and he escaped from the city. However, once he began to love Delilah and to break his sacred trust, the Spirit was withdrawn from him. Personal sin leads to immense foolishness, and it is astonishing that though Samson repeatedly proved Delilah to be a shameless liar, yet he still trusted his secret to her. This is the story of life today in the case of some believers. Though they prove the painful spiritual consequence of investing in worldly things, yet they are repeatedly drawn back to the very same sins.

An even more bewildering parallel is seen in the way some evangelicals in apostate Western denominations commit themselves to close fellowship with Bible deniers, when it has been endlessly proved that they cannot be trusted.

Samson surrendered his purity, obedience and mission to a Philistine woman, and became a broken man. The enemy took him and gouged out his eyes. He lost his moral strength, his physical strength, his dignity, his ministry, and his liberty, becoming a captive animal, humiliated and taunted. Yet, in a painful way, he was still a living lesson to the Israelites. As he formerly constituted a picture of faith, intended to challenge and rebuke their sin and complacency, so now he illustrated the result of their idolatry and impurity. Did the people of Israel see themselves in his fall?

Why did God let Samson fall into sin and incur such a punishment? Because all generations of His people must learn that a holy God must judge even His own people for their sins. Those who *have* been faithful and fruitful must nevertheless come under God's chastisement if they renounce their first love, lose their priorities and yield to compromise with the world and sin.

The severe punishment of Samson is further evidence that he had previously been a holy and faithful man who loved his Lord, and kept His law. If Samson had *always* been sensual, selfish and irresponsible (as modern approach exegetes outrageously claim) would God have blessed him so marvellously one moment and punished him so terribly the next? We surely learn that he was in error only during the last portion of an otherwise faithful life, and that is why he still qualified for the hall of fame of the heroes of faith.

The doctrine of the perseverance of the saints shines like a jewel at the end of Samson's life, assuring us that God never finally rejects His true children. The fallen judge is moved to the most earnest repentance in a cry similar to the prayer of the dying thief at Calvary, 'O Lord God, remember me.' This was a plaintive, humble appeal, not for life or liberty, but for vindication in the sight of the Philistines, that he might give one last demonstration of the glory and power of God. His earthly sight was dark, but he knew that he would see again on entering the spiritual land of Abraham, Isaac, Jacob, Moses, and Joshua, and supremely, he would see the Angel of the Lord Who had appeared to his parents, and Who had commanded him in the days of his power. The Lord heard his cry, forgave his sin, and used him to strike that great, final blow against the wickedness and idolatry of the Philistines. Then was the contrast revealed once more between Samson in his prime, and the general Israelite population!

He was full of faith and boldness.
They were timid and fearful.

He looked to the promised seed, and beyond to the eternal city.
They desired only their present national liberty.

He was free and uninhibited.
They were dominated by the whims of the Philistines.

He was taken note of, and held in awe by the Philistines.
They were despised, and accorded no respect.

He demonstrated the power of God to accomplish things far beyond ordinary human capacity.
They, despite being so numerous, could accomplish nothing.

Finally, *he*, in the time of his punishment and distress, repented and recommitted himself to God.
They remained obdurate in their decadence for forty years.

Sadly, all these comparisons may be applied in great measure to many periods of church history including our own, for the Israelites illustrated the future churches of Christ in bad times. So the record challenges churches languishing in compromise, when their members indulge in worldly things, her worship becoming polluted, and her great exploits of active witness and soul-winning are abandoned.

However, the table of contrasting characteristics just described is destroyed by modern approach expositors, because to them Samson was in many respects as bad as his nation. If we dismiss the information of *Hebrews 11*, we dismiss also the Lord's intended pastoral application to the church of Christ, and yet another book of the Bible falls to vapid, unapplied preaching.

The Samson chapters are given to show that when the *faith* of *Hebrews 11* prevails, then weaknesses are replaced through the Spirit by the opposite strengths. These are surely the themes we must derive and preach from these passages. It should be apparent that to denigrate the judges and to dismiss Samson as a man of his age, as many do, is to destroy the divine purpose behind such chapters.

The message to evangelicals who succumb to modern approach interpretation is that a little liberalism takes more than a portion from God's Word – it takes all its message and usefulness. When shall we see an end of this tendency to depict Samson stamping about in uncontrollable rages, or driven by lust and doing irresponsible things in the name of the Lord? The *Book of Judges* reveals each commentator's work – of what sort it is.

In the event, the last act of Samson probably did break through to the minds and hearts of the people to a marked degree, contributing, we may suppose, to the new desire that took them to Samuel, pleading for his prayers at Mizpeh, a plea which led to their complete deliverance.

This overview is primarily intended to demonstrate the importance of the traditional approach to exposition, which recognises that the biblical history is given for the edification, challenge and comfort of believers in subsequent ages. But readers may want to know what to make of the disastrous closing chapters.

Just as modern evangelical writers ruin the *Book of Judges* by throwing away *Hebrews 11,* and viewing the judges as spiritually backward characters, so they spoil the book by forcing upon it a climax of wickedness and failure. The traditional view – easily proved correct – is that the final chapters belong to the early part of the book, but are placed at the end for good reason. Modern writers make no attempt to debate the evidence for the traditional view, and one is forced to wonder if their extensive study of critical, unbelieving, liberal scholarship has left them unaware of the great commentators and exegetes of former times.

Needless to say, the mistaken view that the period of the judges was a failure considerably affects the message. With such a view we may, for example, prefer the monarchy to the theocracy, giving ample justification today for denominationalism above independency. The message would then run along these lines: The 'independent churches' of the time of the judges failed, and needed to be rescued by the episcopal (or other denominational) 'church' of the monarchy.

It is not our purpose in this book to discuss church organisation, but to provide an example of how seriously faulty exposition may provide faulty guidance for matters of great importance. The rash, brash conclusions of the modern approach ruin the message and application of all historical books, which is not surprising, given its liberal, critical roots. We invite readers to consult the reasons why we affirm that the last chapters of *Judges* speak of the period *before* the judges in Appendix II. Also in this appendix a summary of useful facts about *Judges* is provided.

15
Epilogue

THE BURDEN of this book has been to alert Bible-loving people to the sad decline in standards of biblical interpretation. We have tried to include positive counsel and stimulation, but alas, the unhappy task of showing what is going wrong may have overwhelmed it. We pay tribute to the very many preachers who have seen the shortcomings of the modern approach, and have searched out for themselves a more biblical way. We also salute writers who have issued books on preaching Christ in the Old Testament, and similar themes, providing welcome shafts of light typical of the traditional evangelical approach.

However, the teaching of the modern approach in seminaries shows no signs of weakening. In the US, the bestowing of doctoral degrees continues apace for scholars who advance the cause of this hermeneutical juggernaut. Why should it be thought worthy by evangelical seminaries to celebrate a lifeless, Spirit-quenching, message-destroying school of interpretation, built ultimately on Bible-denying, liberal philosophy? Should we not be able to look to evangelical scholars for guidance of the kind and quality provided by the nineteenth-century divine Patrick Fairbairn? Why is there no modern guide on all the legitimate types of the Old Testament? And would it not be a tremendous boon to preachers to have a thorough guide to and identification of pastoral parallels in the Old Testament? In the course of this book we have referred to Old Testament quotations in the New as a necessary source of information for our 'interpretive grid' of sound expectations. Why has no one in recent times attempted a high quality treatment of these? What a wonderful and rewarding task this would be for a good scholar intent on making a worthy contribution to the studies and message-preparation of working pastors!

If it is good to get help from mortal men, why not research the outstanding preachers and commentators of the past, presenting *their* hermeneutical approaches, rather than those of unbelieving critics? In the event, modern approach writers seldom even acknowledge the post-Reformation interpretive tradition. A work on the methods of Spurgeon alone would probably sell ten times more books than all modern hermeneutics volumes put together, and how highly valued such a work would be! However, these examples only touch the surface of possibilities.

In vain do we look today for *real* evangelical scholarship demonstrating a profound knowledge of the Word combined with a desire to advance preaching. Instead the new approach authors painfully follow each other down the road of modern hermeneutics rooted in Schleiermacher, then Gadamar, then a host of philosophers, rather than faithful theologians.

Some modern evangelical authors are undoubtedly brilliant men, but how we wish they would break free from a system which is crushing the life and fire out of the pulpit. Is it a case of the desire for academic acceptance prevailing over the divine purpose of preaching?

To the church officers we visualised at the opening of this book we say – pray for a preacher who will bring the intended message of the living Word, unrestricted by unspiritual inhibitions, to the hearts and minds of the congregation. Beware of the modern approach and be very careful with seminaries that advocate its restricting of the pastoral purpose of the sacred text. Value instead the great evangelical tradition articulated at the Reformation, espoused by the Puritans, practised in times of great revivals, loved by Victorian preachers, and perpetuated today by numerous 'old order' ambassadors of Calvary throughout the world. Only with this will congregations be fed with the sincere milk of the Word in such a way that they will not need either charismatic pseudo-wonders or musical entertainment to lift their spirits. Only with this will we see powerful conversions, deepened believers, renewed service for Christ, increasing delight in the Word and a restoration of sincerity and vigour in the church, so that Christ will be all and in all.

Thy word is true from the beginning: and every one of thy righteous judgments endureth for ever
Psalm 119.160.

APPENDIX I
Twenty-One Steps for Message Preparation

T HE FOLLOWING suggested steps provide a structured approach for the study and application of a text for ministry to believers. A rather different approach is helpful for preparing evangelistic ministry,[*] and further 'rules' are necessary for prophetic passages and types of Christ. These steps are not so much rules of interpretation, as a general scheme or method of approach. They include some which serve as regulators or checks on oneself, to help keep clear of certain pitfalls.

1 *Read the entire chapter or episode* carefully and more than once, until a clear view is possessed. If necessary resort to commentaries even at this early stage, but only to gain general clarity on the main theme of the narrative, and to clear up obscurities. The time for more detailed reference to commentaries should ideally be later, after one's own mind has been obliged to work. (It is good practice

---

[*]See *Physicians of Souls*, Peter Masters, Wakeman Trust, 2002, pp183-192.

to make sure one knows how to pronounce correctly all the names in the chapter, for it is surprising how overall perception is dulled when the mind stumbles over names.)

2 *Ask – What is going on?* What is the literal, obvious event or theme? Who is doing what, and with what objective? What point is being argued or presented? What historical events are being described? It is important to write down a summary. An explicit or implicit spiritual message or application may immediately occur to us, but for the present, we should rein back the inclination to come to a firm view, and seek to understand fully the outward aspects of the narrative or passage.

In the case of direct teaching, such as that of New Testament epistles, the outward theme and the spiritual message are usually the same, and the objective of our study is to establish that main theme, and why it needed to be said.

3 *Ask – What is the general context?* While still considering the passage at 'face value', the historical and circumstantial context must be taken in view. The assistance of commentaries or an historical survey will be needed. The context will frequently provide an explanation of attitudes and events, showing, for example, whether actions were justified or not. It may show what previous steps the Lord had taken to influence the people. It will provide the background to, say, the pleadings of a psalm. It will not only throw important light on the passage, but will often provide valuable descriptive information for use in the sermon.

4 *Establish the dates and the places.* This is strictly part of the previous rule, but it is sufficiently important to be accorded a distinctive place. The Bible teacher must never work in an historical and geographical fog. Such information should not intrude too

much into the finished address, but all preparation should be anchored to clear notions of when and where things occurred, or were said.

5 *Compare scriptures.* The crucial rule of *1 Corinthians 2.13* must now be applied, and parallel passages and other scriptures which throw light on the text must be referred to. The final address should certainly not flit round all these passages, so that the sermon is an irritating patchwork-quilt of texts, but they must influence our understanding. The consulting of other scriptures is first honoured by an 'analogy of faith' check, meaning that our understanding of the passage, as it develops, must be in harmony with all the principal doctrines of the faith derived from the Word.

Then we seek out passages which interpret or clarify our chosen text. We have already noted several times that our preaching from *Judges* should be governed by *Hebrews 11*, which tells us that the judges were spiritual and faithful men who understood that a Saviour would come in the future. Similarly, preaching on Elijah will be guided by the words of James. Sadly, most recent Bible commentaries ignore New Testament comments made on Old Testament texts.

6 *Identify problems in the passage,* and solve them. Take particular care to resolve any difficult phrases, apparent contradictions, seemingly unfair elements, and other matters which present a stumbling-block to the understanding, and sometimes even to faith. Often such difficulties are the teacher's friends. As he explains them, he gains the attention of his hearers and the whole message is made more effective. For the preacher's own benefit, confusing verses must be cleared up, or he will not be fully equipped to search out the spiritual purpose of the passage. As a general rule, we depend on the older commentators for solving Old Testament problem verses. (Matthew Poole, for example, is extraordinary for the number of

problem texts he resolves in his terse comments.)

7 *Identify key words, and their meanings.* Preparing ministry is not simply a word game. The identifying of key words is not a matter of picking out a few words, each of which will suggest a topic. Nevertheless, some words will clearly have leading significance. Sometimes these may be used repeatedly in a passage, as if the Lord intends them to be noted. It is as though they are underscored. There are nearly always verbs and nouns which we need to explore further. If we are not conversant with the Hebrew or Greek, we will need to consult a concordance-dictionary, such as *Strong's Exhaustive.* Some words almost always need clarifying. (For example, what kind of 'evil' does the text refer to? Is it moral evil, or is it harm and damage?)

It is not necessarily a good short-cut to use a modern translation to throw light on word meanings, although this can be stimulating. The trouble is that modern versions frequently use weaker and less precise words in exchange for the dated but more appropriate words chosen by the *KJV* and sometimes they paraphrase using way off-line synonyms. Much may be lost to the teacher if key words are not checked against the original. Equally, the tense must always be checked in the New Testament by consulting the original Greek or a commentary.

8 *Search for the pastoral significance.* This is the most important stage of preparation – the examination of the passage for its intended spiritual message. The sermon will not yet be shaped, nor the application finally chosen, but all possible applications, implicit and explicit, should be identified. Both the authority for, and the nature of, this inspection come from the same three New Testament texts considered earlier in this book.

Romans 15.4 instructs us to look at passages for examples or doctrines or promises which promote patience, comfort and hope (anticipation of future blessing). 'For whatsoever things were written aforetime were written for our learning, that we through patience and comfort of the scriptures might have hope.'

1 Corinthians 10.1-12 (especially verses 6 and 11) instructs us to identify examples of sin, disobedience, lack of faith, compromise and murmuring (see the longer list on page 36). It also instructs us to focus on faith and victory. We are to treat the passage as though it has been specifically written to teach Gospel-age congregations such spiritual lessons. We are to identify figures of Christ and of Calvary; of grace and of salvation.

2 Timothy 3.16 adds further to this growing 'check list' of expectations and presuppositions which we bring to bear on the passage in our search for pastoral application. We should ask: Is there a doctrine in the text, whether of God, or of man, or of the church? Is there reproof? Is there correction? Is there help in the cultivation of righteousness? Is there a duty taught? Is there instruction on church order and methods?

The three texts we have cited indicate the message-laden purpose of the Scriptures, and tell us that our preparation must include a major investment of effort to identify the pastoral and applicatory lessons intended by God in every passage. According to Paul in *2 Timothy 3.16-17* there is a complete and sufficient set of instructions to bring about the sanctification of God's people in all Scripture, that is, in both Testaments. Do we see these instructions in our preparation? A formal list based on the expectations of these three texts is shown on page 38. We repeat our recommendation that preachers keep such a list or 'grid' in their Bibles. The use of such a list in sermon preparation soon becomes second nature, the user becoming increasingly adept at recognising the message-features mentioned by the apostle.

A warning is necessary if this process is to be carried out

effectively. With a few notable exceptions, the majority of Bible commentators do not search the text for such applications. This is not usually their aim. Their chosen task is to expound the outward, technical sense of the text, in its historical context. Some furnish a handful of rather obvious applicatory observations along the way, but no more than that. Unless a preacher possesses the older and homiletical type of commentary, he will have only slender help in the researching of the pastoral and spiritual purposes of the text.

With or without help we must take pastoral expectations to our chosen passage, and make a rigorous but honest search. It is an essential early part of preparation, and a part which the Lord of the Word delights to bless.

9 *Identify the main subject.* Once the passage has been researched for its spiritual potential, an attempt must be made to establish the chief or overriding point. Is it salvation, or the sin of believers, and if the latter, then which sin in particular? Or is it faith, or encouragement? Or which doctrine is taught? It may be difficult to decide which is the principal topic or theme, for several may jostle for attention. It is important to establish or select an overriding subject of prime importance, otherwise we shall have a headless, meandering message. A sermon should be built around a main point or thrust.

10 *Identify subordinate subjects and principles.* Because the Bible is God's Word, it is profound, teeming with pearls, and nuggets of gold. Alongside the main theme there may be numerous arguments, statements and observations which in their own right express deep matters. We should identify all these 'lesser' statements – often containing promises, doctrines, truths – in the passage. One benefit of examining these is that sometimes one of them emerges as a challenger to our chosen main theme. Equally, the

subordinate ideas may explain and expand the main theme.

11 *Consider the manner of application.* Armed with a main subject and subordinate truths, how are these to be arranged for use? Does the passage itself provide a natural arrangement either by the sequence of events, heads of argument, or evident points? An historical event often consists of an obvious sequence of events, and there may be some form of appeal to those involved, together with a response (for better or worse), and an outcome. It may be possible, in the sermon, for the application to track the stages of an event. (By application we mean such things as – doctrines to be taught; exalting views of Christ to be conveyed; duties to be set forth; challenges to be given; and personal counsels and exhortations to be made.) Alternatively, it may be better to deal with the passage in one run as a single historical event, and then to devote the remainder of the time to application. Either way, the passage must be allowed, wherever possible, to dictate or mould the 'style' of the sermon. If the Holy Spirit has chosen to communicate a spiritual message through an Old Testament event, we should respect His chosen vehicle of presentation. A dramatic event should not be turned into a set of dry propositions. In the case of a New Testament parable, the story form should not be set aside. So we must search and see whether there is a route for application suggested by the passage.

12 *Determine the layout of the address.* The plan of the address should now be devised. How many points will it have? Is a 'background' introduction appropriate? Is there an element of surprise, or some other special characteristic in the passage, which should be represented? Will we narrate an event? Will the sections or points of the sermon be equal proportions of the whole? Where will examples and illustrations be best employed? Will the address adhere to the main topic, with the points supported by reference to

the passage, or will it be passage-focused, with the application drawn from the passage? Such decisions must be consciously made, and not emerge accidentally, because this will lead to a muddled delivery.

13 *Further consulting of commentaries.* In earlier stages commentaries and other resources will have been utilised for specific purposes. Now they should be consulted for their detailed treatment and (if included) application of the passage. Why should this be left to such a late stage of preparation? Because if the teacher runs too quickly to the commentaries, his own ability to see the spiritual purpose of the passage will be diminished. He will be inclined to see only what the commentators see. But are they not right? Perhaps, but, as we have noted, they are not usually looking for the spiritual application; it is almost a minor, supplementary consideration for them. However, having carried out steps 1 to 12 with a clear mind, a careful perusal of commentaries may now correct mistakes. Often it will show up some important points we have missed.

14 *Rigorous review – Is the sermon only descriptive?* This is the first of a set of questions to which we must subject our prepared message. Is it mere narrative? Are we only repeating the story? Are we simply telling people what they could perfectly well read for themselves? We must be ruthless with ourselves! Too many sermons are not worthy of the name. They add virtually nothing of substance. What about ours?

15 *Rigorous review – Is the application realistic?* Applications are made, but are they really warranted? Are they really suggested by the passage? Some preachers begin with a text and apply from everywhere but the passage. What about us? Are the applications worthy, sensible, and honouring to Christ?

16 *Rigorous review – Is this my hobby-horse?* Is this a sermon we preach from any number of texts? Do we bring almost everything down to the same issues? Have we made the very same application only recently? When we prepared, did we do justice to the passage, or did we look at it through the spectacles of our pet subject? Are we really seeking and teaching the whole counsel of God?

17 *Rigorous review – Is the sermon well-organised?* Have we achieved an interesting and effective shape or form? Are the points or sections truly consecutive, connected and logical? A haphazard message is an insult to the intelligence of our hearers, and may even strike them as bizarre. A poorly organised message is also more difficult to preach, because ill-connected fragments do not hold together in the preacher's memory.

18 *Rigorous review – Is there remonstration?* Will our message engage and challenge the minds and hearts of hearers? Do we intend only to tell them about something, or do we plan to go further, and urge or persuade them of their duty? As we unfold the spiritual message, will we remonstrate with the people? Or will we encourage them? Does the planned sermon contain practical counsel, showing, for example, how progress in holiness may be helped or hindered? Is the message so presented that hearers will be moved and encouraged to respond?

19 *Rigorous review – Is there too much matter?* This is the great drawback to thorough preparation, and the most painful part of the entire process. If we have been diligent we may have assembled ideal points, but these may be too numerous. Sacrifices will have to be made. Many of our 'best points' may have to go. *Pruning* is the most positive term for this. If the message is too

complex, it will be necessary, and we must not resent this, or decide to prepare less thoroughly in the future.

20 *Rigorous review – Are there too many secondary references?* A sermon is often greatly enhanced by detouring to other scriptures, or by including apt references. But this is often done unnecessarily, so that precious time is lost, the theme of the message is broken, and hearers are overtaxed. Some preachers resort to other texts almost as an affectation. For some it seems to be a kind of nervous escape or reflex. Some rush round so many texts it is hard to know where they are. Still others seem to think that their hearers will not believe that a text is inspired unless they hear a dozen similar ones quoted alongside. How does our message stand in terms of the number of secondary references?

21 *Earnest prayer.* Of course, the period of preparation would have begun in prayer, and prayer would have been made from time to time throughout. Now, before the final notes are penned, all is again brought before the Lord in prayer. It often happens that even while praying for the effect of the message the mind is blessed to see some aspect more clearly, or to realise that a particular line of reasoning or urging must be emphasised. Prayer is both the starting-point and the crowning act of preparation.

Psalm 10.17 is a wonderful prayer-text. 'Lord, thou hast heard the desire of the humble: thou wilt prepare their heart, thou wilt cause thine ear to hear.' Preaching on this, Spurgeon said:

> 'If God has had love enough to prepare your heart to pray, He has grace enough to give you the blessing. Consider the truthfulness and the faithfulness and the goodness of God, and you will see that it is not possible that He should teach a person to pray for a blessing which He will not give. I cannot imagine any one of you tantalising your child by exciting in him a desire that you do not intend to gratify. You find a desire in your heart; the Lord put

that desire there, and for the honour of His infinite majesty, lest
He stain His goodness and dishonour His great name, He must
hear you.'

APPENDIX II
The Closing Chapters of Judges

HAT HAPPENED at the end of the *Book of Judges*? Did matters really descend into the evil and anarchy depicted in the closing chapters? One notable recent evangelical commentator is so certain that they did that he asserts the main purpose of the book is – 'to demonstrate the meaningless-ness of this stage of Israel's development'. In other words, according to this view, the judges were merely makeshift deliverers, being themselves morally and spiritually insubstantial. The land, say the modern approach men, always deteriorated into chaos after each deliverance.

We have already shown that the age of the judges saw far longer periods of tranquillity and blessedness, than misery and wickedness – the very reverse of the situation during the monarchy. What then should we make of the last five chapters, summarised by the words – 'In those days there was no king in Israel: every man did that which was right in his own eyes'? These sorry words point to a time during which there was no authoritative rule in the land, by either kings or judges. We repeat, the sorry picture of apostasy and lawlessness painted in the closing chapters describes the period *just prior* to the inauguration of the judges. We are shown the rapid decline from the time of Joshua and the elders until the beginning of the judges.

The view that these final chapters (17-21) are an appendix, referring to the period immediately before the judges, is the almost universal older view, maintained more recently by exegetes of stature such as C. J. Goslinga, who says emphatically that 'the author does make clear that these events took place virtually at the beginning of the period of the judges.' How could the events of the last five chapters have occurred during the ministry of the last judge, Samuel, without any mention being made in *1 Samuel*? We should remember that the period of the judges ended with victory over the Philistines, involving the first great spiritual reawakening of the Bible.

It is fairly obvious that the narrative marks a dramatic change of style at the end of chapter 16 (Samson's demise). More obvious still is the 'time key' repeated throughout the appendix (and not once mentioned in the main part of the book). No sooner are we into the events of Micah (chapter 17) than this explanatory time key appears in verse 6: 'In those days there was no king in Israel, but every man did that which was right in his own eyes.' The first half of this verse is to be repeated three times in the course of the closing chapters, appearing twice in each of the two events narrated. It identifies a period of lawlessness, during which there was no cohesive national authority, and there never was such a period at the end of the time of the judges, because Samson lived at the same time as Samuel, and Samuel served all the way to Saul. The period with no rule could only have been between the last of Joshua's elders and the first of the judges.

Chapters 17-21 date themselves to the beginning of *Judges* in other ways also. The tribe of the Danites are described as seeking an inheritance for themselves *(Judges 18.1)* which could only have occurred at the beginning of the period. They would certainly not have remained boxed in by the Amorites *(Judges 1.34)* for three centuries, until the end of the time of the judges. Another indication of the time spoken of in the closing chapters is in *Judges 20.28*, where we read that Phinehas the son of Eleazar was still alive and ministering. He is last mentioned in *Joshua 24.33*, and if the events of *Judges 20* came after Samson, he would have been well over 300 years old by that time.

Then why is the record of the dismal period that occurred before the judges placed at the end of the *Book of Judges*? One answer is this: if it had been inserted where it belongs *historically* (say after *Judges 3.4*) then the main theme and message of the book, showing how God mercifully provided deliverers, would have been delayed by five chapters, and thus blunted and marred by a narrative of wretchedness. By its appearing in an appendix, God's deliverance (the main theme) shines out strongly. However, the dismal patch is not discarded.

Memory tags – useful facts about the judges

Having said so much about the message of *Judges*, we append here for interest the key characteristics of this remarkable period of Israel's history:–

- Judges were rulers of the people.
- Of fifteen judges, only eight have their deeds recorded.
- Following the administrations of Moses and Joshua every tribe was left with an hereditary chief or 'prince' for justice and leadership in war, these princes being joined by the chiefs of families for great issues *(Numbers 26, 27; Joshua 7)*. This was truly 'patriarchal government'.

- However, after Joshua there remained no cohesion between the tribes. Their patriarchal government tended to *segregate* rather than *aggregate* them.

- This should not have happened, as they did have a king – for Jehovah was King, present in His 'Palace-Tabernacle'. But the people failed to embrace the glory of their invisible King, a tragic lack of faith which turned them to idols, and also led to their wanting a king like the nations around them.

- Their idolatry was punished by oppression, which in turn was relieved by the provision of deliverers or judges, acting as agents of the invisible King.

- Judges were raised up by God, but in nearly all cases were endorsed by the free choice of the people, Jephthah being a likely example of the mode of appointment for most. Gideon and Samson were, however, appointed directly by the Lord, the latter even before his birth. Judges were not hereditary rulers.

- Judges appear to have had no special income, apart, perhaps, from a share of the spoils of battle.

- Judges had no retinues of courtiers and servants, and no marks or symbols of public dignity. They chiefly maintained a simple lifestyle.

- Judges delivered the people from enemies, destroyed idolatry and promoted the knowledge of God.

- *Jahn's Biblical Archaeology*[*] provides the following significant observation on the period of the judges:

    'The nation in general experienced much more prosperity than adversity in the time of the judges. Their dominion continued 450 years but the whole time of foreign oppression amounts only to

---

[*] *Jahn's Biblical Archaeology*, translated by Thomas C. Upham, Andover, 1839.

111 years, scarcely a fourth part of the period. Even during these 111 years the whole nation was seldom under the yoke at the same time, but for the most part separate tribes only were held in servitude; nor were their oppressions always very severe, and all the calamities terminated in the advantage and glory of the people so soon as they abolished idolatry and returned to their King Jehovah.

'... The Hebrews had no reason to desire a change in their constitution; the only requirement was that they should observe the conditions on which national prosperity was promised them.'

Physicians of Souls
The Gospel Ministry
285 pages, paperback, ISBN 1 870855 34 5

'Compelling, convicting, persuasive preaching, revealing God's mercy and redemption to dying souls, is seldom heard today. The noblest art ever granted to our fallen human race has almost disappeared.'

Even where the free offer of the Gospel is treasured in principle, regular evangelistic preaching has become a rarity, contends the author. These pages tackle the inhibitions, theological and practical, and provide powerful encouragement for physicians of souls to preach the Gospel. A vital anatomy or order of conversion is supplied with advice for counselling seekers.

The author shows how passages for evangelistic persuasion may be selected and prepared. He also challenges modern church growth techniques, showing the superiority of direct proclamation. These and other key topics make up a complete guide to soul-winning.

Worship in the Melting Pot
148 pages, paperback, ISBN 1 870855 33 7

'Worship is truly in the melting pot,' says the author. 'A new style of praise has swept into evangelical life shaking to the foundations traditional concepts and attitudes.' How should we react? Is it all just a matter of taste and age? Will churches be helped, or changed beyond recognition?

This book presents four essential principles which Jesus Christ laid down for worship, and by which every new idea must be judged.

Here also is a fascinating view of how they worshipped in Bible times, including their rules for the use of instruments, and the question is answered – What does the Bible teach about the content and order of a service of worship today?

The Mutual Love of Christ and His People

An explanation of the *Song of Solomon* for personal devotions and Bible study groups

115 pages, paperback, ISBN 1 870855 40 X

The courtship of the *Song of Solomon* provides fascinating scenes and events designed to show the love of Christ for His redeemed people, and theirs for Him. Here, also, are lessons for Christians when they become cold or backslidden, showing the way to recover Christ's presence in their lives.

Prophecies of Christ abound in the *Song*, together with views of the bride's destiny, as she prepares to cross the mountains into eternal glory, where the greatest wedding of all will take place.

This book begins with a brief overview of the reasons why the *Song* should be seen as allegorical – the viewpoint held throughout church history by the overwhelming majority of preachers and commentators. Then, in verse-by-verse mode, but designed for continuous devotional reading, the symbols are explained and applied.

Testimonies to the blessing obtained through this treatment of the *Song* have come from all over the world, from ministers and 'lay' people alike.

God's Rules for Holiness

139 pages, paperback, ISBN 1 870855 37 X

Taken at face value the Ten Commandments are binding on all people, and will guard the way to Heaven, so that evil will never spoil its glory and purity. But the Commandments are far greater than their surface meaning, as this book shows.

They challenge us as Christians on a still wider range of sinful deeds and attitudes. They provide positive virtues as goals. And they give immense help for staying close to the Lord in our walk and worship.

The Commandments are vital for godly living and for greater blessing, but we need to enter into the panoramic view they provide for the standards and goals for redeemed people.

Heritage of Evidence

127 pages, paperback, ISBN 1 870855 39 6

In today's atheistic climate most people have no idea how much powerful evidence exists for the literal accuracy and authenticity of the biblical record. The British Museum holds a huge number of major discoveries that provide direct corroboration and background confirmation for an immense sweep of Bible history. This survey of Bible-authenticating exhibits has been designed as a guide for visitors, and also to give pleasure and interest to readers unable to tour the galleries. It will also be most suitable for people who need to see the accuracy and inspiration of the Bible.

The 'tour' followed here started life over forty years ago and has been used by many thousands of people including youth and student groups.

Almost every item viewed on the tour receives a full colour photograph. Room plans are provided for every gallery visited showing the precise location of artefacts, and time-charts relate the items to contemporary kings and prophets. The book is enriched by pictures and descriptions of famous 'proofs' in other museums.

Only One Baptism of the Holy Spirit

109 pages, paperback, ISBN 1 870855 17 5

Young Christians these days are confronted by much confusion on the teaching of the Holy Spirit and how He baptises, fills and anoints God's people. Contradictory statements and clashing ideas flow from a new generation of anecdotal-style books.

When is the believer baptised with the Spirit, and what does it amount to? Is there a second baptism? How exactly does the Spirit witness with our spirit? How does assurance come? Is the believer to struggle against sin, or does the Lord fight the battle for him? What is the filling of the Spirit? Clear answers are given to all such questions, with 'proof texts'. Ideal for all, especially young believers and study groups.

Do We Have a Policy?
For church health and growth
93 pages, paperback, ISBN 1 870855 30 2

What are our aims for the shaping of our church fellowship, and for its growth? Do we have an agenda or framework of desired objectives?

The apostle Paul had a very definite policy, and called it his 'purpose', using a Greek word which means – a plan or strategy displayed for all to see.

This book sets out ten policy ideals, gleaned from Paul's teaching, all of which are essential for the health and growth of a congregation today.

The Lord's Pattern for Prayer
118 pages, paperback, ISBN 1 870855 36 1

Subtitled – 'Studying the lessons and spiritual encouragements in the most famous of all prayers.' This volume is almost a manual on prayer, providing a real spur to the devotional life. The Lord's own plan and agenda for prayer – carefully amplified – takes us into the presence of the Father, to prove the privileges and power of God's promises to those who pray.

Chapters cover each petition in the Lord's Prayer. Here, too, are sections on remedies for problems in prayer, how to intercede for others, the reasons why God keeps us waiting for answers, and the nature of the prayer of faith.

Men of Purpose
197 pages, illustrated, paperback, ISBN 1 870855 41 8

The Healing Epidemic
227 pages, paperback, ISBN 1 870855 00 0

Steps for Guidance
184 pages, paperback, ISBN 1 870855 19 1

The Charismatic Phenomenon *[co-authored with John C. Whitcomb]*
113 pages, paperback, ISBN 1 870855 01 9

www.wakemantrust.org